INTRODUCING

Critical Theory

Stuart Sim • Borin Van Loon

Edited by Richard Appignanesi

Icon Books UK ◤◢ Totem Books USA

This edition published in the UK
in 2004 by Icon Books Ltd.,
The Old Dairy, Brook Road,
Thriplow, Royston SG8 7RG
email: info@iconbooks.co.uk
www.iconbooks.co.uk

Sold in the UK, Europe, South Africa
and Asia by Faber and Faber Ltd.,
3 Queen Square, London WC1N 3AU
or their agents

Distributed in the UK, Europe, South
Africa and Asia by TBS Ltd., Frating
Distribution Centre, Colchester Road,
Frating Green, Colchester CO7 7DW

This edition published in Australia in
2004 by Allen and Unwin Pty. Ltd.,
PO Box 8500, 83 Alexander Street,
Crows Nest, NSW 2065

Previously published in the UK and
Australia in 2001

This edition published in the USA
in 2005 by Totem Books
Inquiries to: Icon Books Ltd.,
The Old Dairy, Brook Road,
Thriplow, Royston
SG8 7RG, UK

Distributed to the trade in the USA by
National Book Network Inc.,
4720 Boston Way, Lanham,
Maryland 20706

Distributed in Canada by
Penguin Books Canada,
10 Alcorn Avenue, Suite 300,
Toronto, Ontario M4V 3B2

ISBN 1 84046 588 3

Printed and bound in Singapore
by Tien Wah Press Ltd.

The Theory of Everything

Theory has become one of the great growth areas in cultural analysis and academic life over the last few decades. It is now taken for granted that theoretical tools can be applied to the study of, for example, texts, societies, or gender relations.

The phenomenon of "cultural studies" in general, one of the major success stories of interdisciplinary enquiry, is based on just that assumption.

Any area of our culture is amenable to the application of the latest theories.

The further assumption is being made that the application of such theories will lead to a significant increase in understanding of how our culture works.

The Grand Narrative of Marxism

The motivation for this development can be traced back to the rise of Marxism. **Karl Marx** (1818–83) and his followers bequeathed us an all-embracing theory, or "grand narrative" as it is more commonly referred to nowadays.

IT'S ABOUT TIME VAN LOON DID A NEW DRAWING OF ME...

You can analyse and form value judgements on any cultural phenomenon: literature, art, music, political systems, sport, race relations, etc.

Entire cultures can be put under the microscope of Marxist theory. It forms a paradigm of the way in which any critical theory in general works. Cultural artefacts are tested against the given projection of the world as it is, or should be, constructed.

The Politics of Criticism

One criticism levelled against critical theory says that it is an "alternative metaphysics", promoting a particular world view, and, at least implicitly, a particular politics. There is nothing intrinsically wrong with such a procedure, as long as it is made clear what that metaphysics entails. What is it trying to achieve? One can then accept or reject its programme.

From Marxism onwards, critical theory has been very closely linked to political positions.

Nor that critical theory should be kept separate from the world of politics.

We cannot assume that any criticism is a "value-free" activity.

A great deal of its value stems from its ability to remain politically engaged. Being critical is being political: it represents an intervention into a much wider debate than the aesthetic alone, and that is surely something to be encouraged. We live in politically interesting times, after all.

5

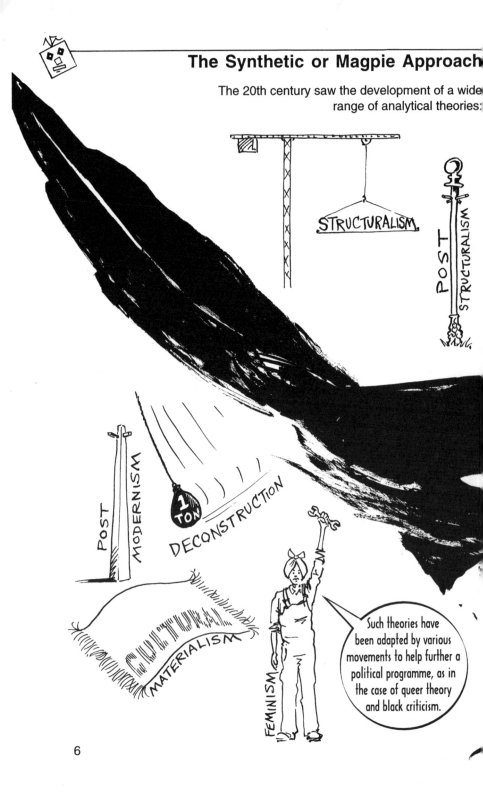

The 20th century saw the development of a wide range of analytical theories:

STRUCTURALISM

POST STRUCTURALISM

POST MODERNISM

1 TON

DECONSTRUCTION

CULTURAL MATERIALISM

FEMINISM

Such theories have been adapted by various movements to help further a political programme, as in the case of queer theory and black criticism.

The cultural analyst can pick or mix from the catalogue of theories to put together synthetic models for whatever the task may happen to be.

> Feminism can be crossed with Marxism or deconstruction; Marxism with postmodernism, poststructuralism, or postcolonialism – and so on in a variety of permutations.

LAST POST COLONIALISM

Except for the most committed enthusiasts of particular movements, most critics tend to operate in magpie fashion these days, selecting a bit of this theory and a bit of that for their own personalized approach.

> The sheer profusion of theories with which we are confronted promotes this kind of experiment.

> In the theory world at present, it is very much a consumer's market.

Bringing Theory to the Surface

To be a critic now, especially in academic life, is also to be a theorist – as any student in the humanities and social sciences will be only too painfully aware.

One no longer studies "literature", but literature plus the full range of critical theories used to construct readings of narratives.

The same thing goes for art history, media studies, sociology – and so on through the humanities and social sciences.

Cultural studies ranges over many of these disciplines.

How we arrive at value judgements, and, indeed, whether we **can** arrive at value judgements, are now at least as important considerations as **what** the actual value judgements themselves are.

Hidden Agendas and Ideologies

Of course, theories have always operated "under the surface", prior to the development of the term "critical theory" itself, but they were generally implicit rather than explicit.

It was a case of assumptions that were taken for granted rather than used in a self-conscious way.

Liberal humanists tended to assume the "ennobling power" of great literature, for example; New Critics in the 1940s and 50s assumed that literary artefacts featured an "organic unity" – the higher the order of organic unity, the greater the work.

"Assumptions that are taken for granted" is a pretty good and handy definition of ideology.

Theoretical Reflexivity

Self-consciousness, or "reflexivity" as we now call it, in the application of theory is what defines the current state of play in the various disciplines of the humanities and social sciences. A student preparing a dissertation or thesis will normally be advised to outline the theoretical model being used, first of all, before going on to undertake the actual task of analysis itself.

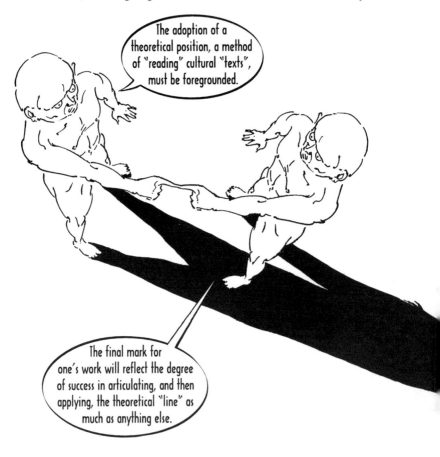

The last thing one wants to be accused of in such situations is being "undertheorized" – that way, low marks lie. The successful student in higher education reaches theoretically-informed conclusions in essays and exams, and can show precisely how the theory informed those conclusions.

Science Studies: the Paradigm Model

But it is not only in the humanities and social sciences that critical theory is deployed. Even the hard sciences have been infiltrated to some extent. Science as a social phenomenon is most certainly a target for critical theory. One well-known founder of "science studies" is the historian and philosopher of science **Thomas Kuhn** (b. 1922).

Scientific history consists of a series of "scientific revolutions", each instituting a new "paradigm" of thought and practice incommensurable with the old.

Like any other social activity, science is a legitimate topic for the critical theorist to explore.

Science has repaid the compliment by providing critical theory with a whole new range of critical concepts to add to its repertoire.

11

Postmodernism and Science

Postmodernism and poststructuralism, for example, have drawn freely on recent developments in physics to reinforce their world-view, with its emphasis on undecidability, gaps in our knowledge, the pervasive factor of difference and the limitations of our understanding.

Quantum mechanics, chaos theory and complexity theory, in particular, constitute extremely fruitful sources of examples that seem to confirm postmodern "relativism". These sciences suggest that the material world is far less stable, or predictable, than we have traditionally assumed it to be.

Science and critical theory seem in this case to be mutually supportive, but all is not well in this relationship.

he Sokal Scandal

1996, an article by **Alan Sokal** (b. 1955), a professor physics at New York University, appeared in the respected itical theory journal *Social Text*. This article, "Transgressing the Boundaries: Towards a Transformative Hermeneutics of Quantum Gravity", arguing for a postmodern "liberatory" science,

proposed an extreme relativism that was clearly lunatic. Sokal had concocted a deliberate hoax, but the journal editors accepted it as serious research.

For instance, I suggest that pi (π) isn't constant and universal but <u>relative</u> to the position of an observer, and is therefore subject to "ineluctable historicity" ...

... that really should have alerted the suspicions of anyone responsibly competent!

okal at once revealed s hoax to the press and e scandal became international front-page news. /hat was Sokal trying to do?

In Defence of Big Science

Sokal tells us in a book published with Jean Bricmont, *Intellectual Impostures: Postmodern Philosophers' Abuse of Science* (1997). The hoax served to expose the pretentious and amateurish misuse of recent physics by leading French theorists, Derrida, Lyotard, Baudrillard and Kristeva. Sokal provided deadly ammunition to the fundamentalists of "Big Science" who reject any hint that science might be "socially constructed".

The notion of a "postmodern science" is entirely illicit.

Science cannot be appropriated to the relativist views of critical theory. The issue remains – is science purely autonomous or "constructed" like everything else cultural?

Misappropriations of scientific concepts have occurred in critical theory, that's true; but is it also true, as Big Science defenders argue, that postmodern theorists are deeply hostile to genuine scientific methods and progress itself?

How did we arrive at this situation where theory plays such a critical role? And what theories do we need to be most aware of in our approach to cultural study nowadays? Let's start with the "grand narrative" known as Marxism, which has always aspired to be a universal explanatory theory.

MARXISM

A Theory For All Seasons

Marxism analyses all phenomena in terms of its theory of <u>dialectical materialism</u> ...

And a particular historical vision accompanies this theory.

We might think of Marxism as a "theory for all seasons", prepared to comment on anything and everything, at all times and in all places.

Origins of Marxism

The immediate source of Marxian dialectical materialism is found in the idealist philosophy of **G.W.F. Hegel** (1770–1831). Hegel enriched theory with the crucial term, **alienation**, which explains the interrelation of **logic** to **history**. In logic, it specifies the contradiction latent in all thinking, meaning that one idea will inevitably provoke its opposite. Hegel's aim was to resolve this in and by **consciousness** itself …

… a proof of God's existence **THESIS** *gives rise to a disproof …* ? **— ANTITHESIS — SYNTHESIS**

Consciousness proceeds in this way historically to a higher synthesis, in a continuous upward spiral of <u>self-realization.</u>

Alienation in this scheme is **dialectical**, that is, the inadequacy of one form of consciousness turns into another, again and again, until a "proper science" is achieved.

16

Absolute Spirit: the Logic of History

Alienation is a process by which mind – as the consciousness of a subject (*thesis*) – becomes an object of thought for itself (*antithesis*). And thereby the human mind constantly progresses to the next higher stage of synthesis and self-consciousness.

To the question – "What is the object of history?" – Hegel's reply is ...

... the realization of absolute knowledge.

History is the journey of the "World Spirit" in its progress through a series of stages until it reaches the highest form of self-realization, **Absolute Spirit**. That form had been attained in Hegel's view by the Prussian state in which he served as a public official (i.e. as professor of philosophy at the University of Berlin.)

The Communist Manifesto

Hegel's dialectic is idealist. Marx gave it a materialist foundation, that is, he shifted alienation away from "mind contemplating itself" to the **class struggle** as the real history of consciousness in progress.

Our task is to contemplate the process of consciousness from the vantage point that it will attain only at the end of its journey – but not to <u>interfere</u> ...

No ... philosophers have only <u>interpreted</u> the world, in various ways; the point, however, is to <u>change</u> it.

quote from Marx, "11th Thesis on Feuerbach" (1845)

The realization of philosophy – literally its *end* – is for Marx the defeat of bourgeois capitalism by the industrial working class, and the establishment of a Communist society which finally abolishes the "latent contradiction" of exploiter and exploited.

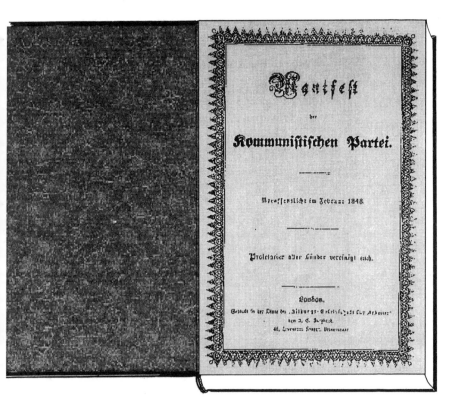

And this is the programme that Marx sets out in
The Communist Manifesto (1848).

18

The history of all hitherto existing society is the history of class struggles. Freeman and slave, patrician and plebeian, lord and serf, guild-master and journeyman, in a word, oppressor and oppressed, stood in constant opposition to one another, carried on an uninterrupted, now hidden, now open fight, a fight that each time ended, either in a revolutionary reconstitution of society at large, or in the common ruin of the contending classes.

Capitalism has simplified the class antagonisms into two great hostile ones – <u>bourgeoisie</u> versus <u>proletariat</u>.

The struggle is reduced to the **private** ownership of the means of production versus the workers who **sell** their labour to this capitalist system of production.

Engels

Marx

THE HIDDEN MECHANISMS OF SOCIETY

How does capitalism "work"? The real (dialectical) question for Marx is: how does it <u>reproduce</u> and maintain itself?

The answer is: by two mechanisms normally camouflaged from view, which it is Marx's aim to expose and bring to revolutionary consciousness. The first mechanism is <u>consumerism</u> ...

A worker's <u>production</u> ...

... depends on his (or her) <u>reproduction</u>.

Food, clothing and shelter for my family.

Work, work, work!

The second mechanism is **surplus value**, by which capitalist production succeeds in exploiting more labour time than is actually paid for. This is a complex analysis from which we need only retain the essential – the hidden, disguised or **unconscious** nature of the system at work.

Infra- and Super-structures

There is a third hidden structure which is general and fundamental to all societies, including the capitalist. Society always consists of an economic base or **infrastructure**, and a **superstructure**. The superstructure comprises everything *cultural* – religion, politics, law, education, the arts, etc. – which is determined by a specific economy (slave-based, feudal, mercantile, capitalist etc.).

Understand the superstructure as <u>ideology</u> - ways of thinking characteristic of class behaviour (what we "take for granted" as natural).

What ideology is literally *based* on is the economic infrastructure – the means by which it **produces** itself, its wealth, and who **owns** those means of production.

Once again, we notice Marx's critical insistence on the hidden: religion, politics, law, etc. – everything cultural that we "live by" – disguises and renders perfectly natural an economic means of production that is unnatural.

Economic Determinism

In the strict, or what is often called the "crude", view of Marxism, the ideologies of culture (like art) are by-products determined by the economic base.

How **much**, to what **degree**, is culture economically determined?

This has been a considerable source of debate in Marxist circles. Some theorists conjecture that certain activities in the superstructure – most notably the arts – might have a "relative autonomy" from the base.

Did a slave-labour economy directly "produce" Greek art?

Not quite so simply. It is only "in the last instance" that the economy dictates superstructural activity.

But what exactly does "relative autonomy" or "in the last instance" mean? Such debates in critical theory are important in deciding whether or not we can simply "read off" events in the superstructure from events in the economic infrastructure.

22

The Hidden Text

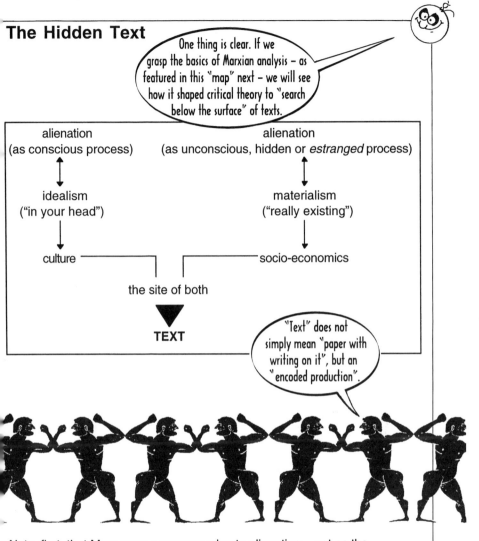

One thing is clear. If we grasp the basics of Marxian analysis – as featured in this "map" next – we will see how it shaped critical theory to "search below the surface" of texts.

alienation
(as conscious process)

alienation
(as unconscious, hidden or *estranged* process)

idealism
("in your head")

materialism
("really existing")

culture ——————————————————— socio-economics

the site of both

▼

TEXT

"Text" does not simply mean "paper with writing on it", but an "encoded production".

Note, first, that Marx gave a new meaning to alienation – not as the Hegelian process of self-consciousness but as an unconscious **estrangement** from oneself determined by one's class condition (= false consciousness).

The inheritances of Marxism in critical theory are:

1. Tension of idealism versus materialism (the autonomy versus social construction of a text).
2. A hidden or camouflaged unconscious.
3. Interventionism: a sense that critical theory *can* make a difference.

Mapping the Origins of Critical Theory

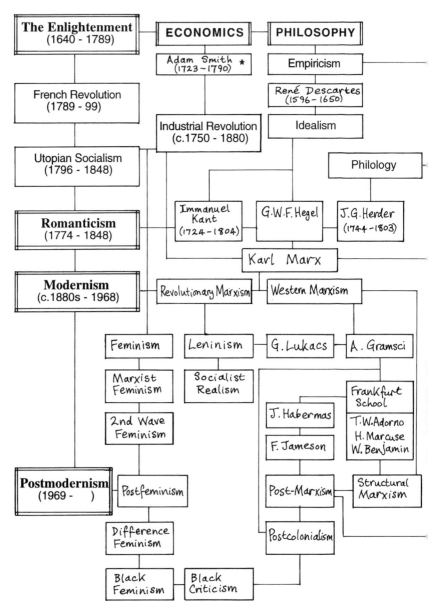

* *Single names given in the table are 'representative figures'*

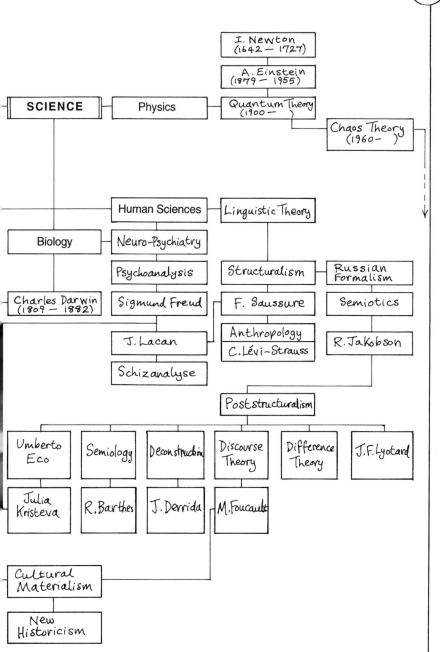

SCIENCE — Physics — I. Newton (1642 – 1727)

A. Einstein (1879 – 1955)

Quantum Theory (1900 –)

Chaos Theory (1960 –)

SCIENCE — Human Sciences — Linguistic Theory

Biology — Neuro-Psychiatry

Psychoanalysis — Structuralism — Russian Formalism

Charles Darwin (1809 – 1882) — Sigmund Freud — F. Saussure — Semiotics

J. Lacan — Anthropology C. Lévi-Strauss — R. Jakobson

Schizanalyse

Poststructuralism

Umberto Eco — Semiology — Deconstruction — Discourse Theory — Difference Theory — J.F. Lyotard

Julia Kristeva — R. Barthes — J. Derrida — M. Foucault

Cultural Materialism

New Historicism

For all its apparently monolithic character...

SCHOOLS OF MARXISM

...Marxism has managed to generate several distinct and opposed schools of critical theory. The question of how economic base and superstructure interact is often at the root of such disagreements.

The concept of "Western Marxism" was devised to distinguish the way Marxism developed in the advanced industrial societies of Western Europe ...

... and to a certain extent in North America.

Different from its Soviet or Maoist (that is, "Eastern") form, in which an extreme socialism was actually put into practice.

Often criticized for its academic bias, Western Marxism (which has many variants) has evinced a particular interest in the superstructure, most notably the arts. In its earliest pre-Western Marxist form, however, Marxist critical theory tended to assume that everything that happened in the superstructure, including the arts, was a mere reflection of what happened in the base.

26

Reflection Theory

The work of the Russian aesthetician **Georgi Plekhanov** (1856–1918) is a good example of crude reflectionism. For Plekhanov, art was a recorder of social developments. By examining the art of a given period, we could pin down that period's ideological character also. This meant that we could indeed "read off" the ideology from the art. If the art was decadent, then it must have been the product of socio-political decadence: a *direct reflection* of it, in fact.

Plekhanov

"Art for art's sake" is an obvious bourgeois phenomenon, since its lack of political content leaves the status quo intact.

ART FOR ART'S SAKE...

MONEY FOR GOD'S SAKE

Anything categorized as following that line, as Cubism (1910–14) was by Plekhanov, must be condemned.

From such a perspective, critical theory became a relatively straightforward exercise, with clearly delineated paths of inquiry. The point was to determine what the art reflected about its society. "Reflection theory" has exercised a powerful hold over Marxist critical practice ever since.

Zhdanovite Socialist Realism

Reflectionist ideas underpin the aesthetic theory later developed under the Soviet political regime, called **Socialist Realism**. It was instituted in 1934 under the watchful eye of Stalin's cultural commissar, the dreaded **A.A. Zhdanov** (1896–1948).

Socialist realism requires creative artists to follow the Communist Party line, to deal only in subjects approved by the Party and display the correct political attitude ...

... the working class are all heroes, capitalists are always evil.

In other words, artists *reflected* social reality as it was ideally conceived of by the Party (and its reading of Marx), and became, in real terms, propagandists for the cause of Communism. To Zhdanov, artists were little better than civil servants – or "engineers of the soul".

28

Art, in this formula, had to be presented in a form accessible to the wider public. This strictly ruled out experiment. Art was no longer to be considered the preserve of an élite with specialized interests separate from the lives of ordinary individuals.

Modernism was effectively banished from the Soviet Union as a result.

We were forced to write, compose, or paint in an academic realist manner that was largely shunned by our peers in the West.

Avant-garde modernism was the dominant aesthetic of the 20th-century capitalist West. Even the mere *suggestion* of such modernism in one's art was enough to bring down the full might of the state machine on your head – as composers such as **Dmitri Shostakovitch** (1906–75) were to discover to their cost.

Shostakovitch

The Battle for Class Consciousness

Western Marxism is generally taken to begin with the work of **Georg Lukács** (1885–1971), whose early writings on philosophy and literature exerted a huge influence on several generations of Western European theorists. Lukács's *History and Class Consciousness* (1923) preached a more humanist approach to class struggle, in comparison to the authoritarian Soviet Union model. Unlike many Soviet thinkers of the time, Lukács did not believe in the "inevitability" of revolution – it had to be consciously striven for through the combined efforts of the working class and the Communist Party in a creative rather than a dogmatic manner.

The glorious struggle of the people's revolution will triumph over the running dogs of bourgeois capitalism. It says here.

A situation in which the "facts" speak out unmistakably for or against a definite course of action has never existed, and neither can nor will exist.

This amounted to a rejection of the deterministic interpretations of Marxist thought so popular in the Party at the time.

30

To orthodox Marxists like **V.I. Lenin** (1870–1924), who already exercised dictatorial powers – extended even further under **Joseph Stalin** (1879–1953) – such views were considered dangerous to the socialist cause.

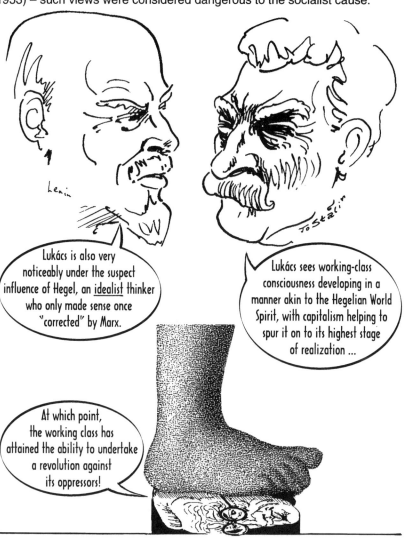

Lukács is also very noticeably under the suspect influence of Hegel, an <u>idealist</u> thinker who only made sense once "corrected" by Marx.

Lukács sees working-class consciousness developing in a manner akin to the Hegelian World Spirit, with capitalism helping to spur it on to its highest stage of realization ...

At which point, the working class has attained the ability to undertake a revolution against its oppressors!

This was far too metaphysical a conception for the Comintern. Lukács was accordingly disciplined and forced to offer a public recantation of the work. *History and Class Consciousness* was later to resurface as a favoured text amongst the student revolutionaries of the 1960s (notably in the 1968 *événements* in Paris).

Lukács's Hegelian roots are also evident in his early work on literature, *Theory of the Novel* (1920). This is still a widely studied text today, and its linking of the novel to the rise of bourgeois culture in Europe has been echoed in various other studies since.

It is now more or less a commonplace to see the novel, in its earliest phase at least, as an expression of bourgeois values ...

With the focus firmly on the individual establishing his or her place in a competitive world.

As I see it, the novel is deeply embedded in the development of modern culture.

Lukács was later to develop a highly controversial theory of novelistic realism, "critical realism", based on the practice of his favourite 19th-century novelists, such as

Sir Walter Scott
(1771–1832),

Honoré de Balzac
(1799–1850),

What can you do with me, Scott? I was a notably conservative, establishment-supporting figure.

and **Count Leo Tolstoy**
(1828–1910).

Regardless of their political outlook, novelists must reveal the pressures working within their society that led to the development of its particular matrix of social relations.

What are the constraints placed on us as individuals within a given social class at a given historical point?

33

A Critical Realist View of Alienation

20th-century novelists who seemed to follow the Lukácsian creed of realism – such as I, <u>Thomas Mann</u> (1875–1955) – were praised by Lukács.

Thos. Mann

Those who present mankind as essentially alienated from each other for <u>metaphysical</u> rather than <u>social</u> reasons – such as I, <u>Franz Kafka</u> (1883–1924) – must be criticized by Lukács.

Kafka.

What I mean is this: "alienation" is not an inescapable "human condition". Kafka believes it is; socialism does not.

"Franz Kafka or Thomas Mann", a chapter title from *The Meaning of Contemporary Realism* (1958), was to become something of a battle cry for Lukács – a political rather than strictly literary choice for the individual to make, whether as author or reader.

Lukács was eventually to condemn modernism in general as presenting a distorted picture of reality which inhibited political action. This viewpoint brought him into dispute with the modernist experimental dramatist and Marxist, **Bertolt Brecht** (1898–1956).

Brecht, backed up by the Marxist critic **Walter Benjamin** (1892–1940), complained that Lukács's conception of realism was far too narrow.

Creative artists must be left free to experiment as the culture around them changes.

To write in the style of 19th-century realism would be to cease being a realist now.

Lukács was unrepentant. He continued to attack modernism and defend his own vision of realism until the very end of his career. Such stalwarts of modernism as **James Joyce** (1882–1941),

Samuel Beckett (1906–89)

and **William Faulkner** (1897–1962) were treated no better than Kafka.

Western Marxism, unlike Lukács, has adopted a much more positive attitude towards the modernist ethic and its major practitioners.

35

The Theory of Hegemony

Marxists have always found it difficult to explain two problems. Both concern the failure of predicting revolution in capitalist societies.

Why do the exploited classes of capitalist society so often seem quite content to go along with the ruling ideology, when it is manifestly not in their best interests to do so?

Why do socialist revolutions fail to materialize in advanced capitalist societies?

These have been vexed questions within the Marxist movement. The concept of **hegemony** was developed to explain away such discrepancies. In the hands of the Italian Marxist, **Antonio Gramsci** (1891–1937), this concept became a sophisticated tool for cultural analysis.

36

Gramsci rejected the crude deterministic notion that the exploited working classes must inevitably recognize revolution as "in their best interests". Marxism had failed to consider how ideology actually works to make itself **unrecognizable** as such (another "disguise"). This is the trick of hegemony …

… to persuade the <u>whole</u> of society that a prevailing ideology – the very one which in fact protects the <u>dominant</u> class – is really the only natural and normal way of thinking.

Power cannot simply depend on repression, but on controlling the <u>power of knowledge</u>.

We will see later how Michel Foucault's "archaeology" of knowledge digs under the apparent layer of hegemonic "consent" to uncover the workings of cultural empowerment – a way already signposted by Gramsci.

Cultural Criticism

Capitalist societies are adept at disseminating their ideological beliefs without having to resort to force. Ideology is passed on at the *level of ideas*, as much as by economic pressures (often unwittingly by the individuals involved).

The arts and the media are critical elements of this process.

This gives added impetus to critical theory as a way of exploring ideology in all its varied manifestations.

Such ideas were later to be developed further by the structural Marxist movement. Some critics began to wonder how we could ever break out of hegemony's embrace, so successful did it seem in maintaining the political status quo and defusing dissent at source.

The Frankfurt School's Critical Theory

Perhaps the most important strand of cultural criticism in Western Marxism was the Frankfurt School. It developed a rigorous approach to cultural analysis, particularly as seen in the work of its major figures, **Theodor Adorno** (1903–69),

Our School gave the name "critical theory" to its method of analysis.

Max Horkheimer (1895–1973),

Note: this book uses <u>critical theory</u> to cover the entire scope of other theories ...

and **Herbert Marcuse** (1898–1979).

Our approach was based in Marxism, but was just as willing to criticize the failings of the Soviet Union as those of Western society.

"Critical theory" is an amalgam of philosophical and social-scientific techniques (often making extensive use of statistical questionnaires in its inquiries) that had wide-ranging applications. Established as a research institute at the University of Frankfurt in the early 1920s, the School fled from Germany on the Nazi takeover in 1933 and subsequently relocated in New York (returning to Frankfurt after the Second World War).

The Progress of Irrationalism

Adorno, Horkheimer and Marcuse challenged entrenched aspects of orthodox Marxist thought – such as the role of the Communist Party and the concept of class. Adorno and Horkheimer's jointly authored *Dialectic of Enlightenment* (1944) even questioned the validity of the Enlightenment project itself, of which Marxism is regarded as a constituent part.

What has the "cult of progress", encouraged by the Enlightenment, actually brought us to in modernity?

Extreme rationality has its dark negative underside of <u>unreason</u>. Look around – the Holocaust's system of mass extermination, the Soviet Union's gulags, the A-bomb annihilation – this is the progress of unreason.

They suspected the falsehood of "grand narratives" 35 years before I did …

We will return later to Jean-François Lyotard's verdict on "grand narratives", but, in the meantime …

Looking round, as the Second World War came to a terrifying savage end, amid the ruins of civilization East and West, Adorno and Horkheimer could see only deeply repressive "administered societies" on each side of the ideological divide – the West being no less culpable in this respect than the Stalinist Soviet Union.

Hegemony in Western civilization had all but destroyed the possibility of political dissent under a glossy appearance of mass culture "consent". This was a theme explored in the work of Marcuse.

Writing in the 1960s, Marcuse recognized a "one-dimensional" society in which the forces of advanced capitalism seemed triumphant over those of the traditional left. Political opposition to capitalism, especially in America where Marcuse remained after the war, had all but been eradicated.

> The bulk of the population can see no real reason to rebel against a system which appears to meet their material needs more than adequately and provide a reasonable "democratic" sense of personal security.

> The alternative offered by the Soviet system seems deeply unattractive.

Marcuse felt that the Marxist category of class had broken down in this situation.

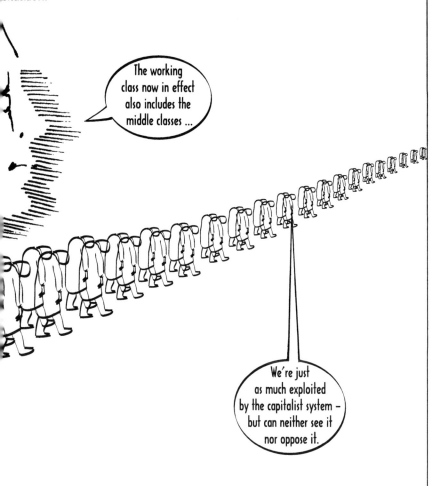

The working class now in effect also includes the middle classes ...

We're just as much exploited by the capitalist system – but can neither see it nor oppose it.

The traditional working class was also in decline, given the speed and scope of technological change now creating a **post-industrial society**, very different to anything that Marx or his immediate disciples could ever have envisaged.

The Alternative or "New Left"

Under such advanced technological circumstances, Marxist thinking could no longer rely on the working class as the saviour of mankind. New constituencies of individuals had to be found to maintain the struggle against capitalism in the name of human liberation.

Students and various minority groups – the black population of America – must replace the working class as the "gravediggers of capitalism".

Marcuse moved away from traditional Marxist notions of how revolution was supposed to come about.

His enthusiastic espousal of the American *counter-culture* (rock 'n' roll, jazz and blues, avant-garde art) signalled a radical break with the orthodox tradition.

Many, especially among the growing student protest movement, find him very appealing.

I was turned into a guru of the "New Left" in its struggle against the established system, the anti-Vietnam war protest, militant student revolution, desegregation and other issues ...

The Politics of Avant-garde Art

Adorno, too, was an articulate theoretical champion of the artistic avant-garde. He was a composer himself and defended the twelve-tone music of **Arnold Schoenberg** (1874–1951) and his disciples, and then later the new German cinema of the 1960s. And he did so for reasons similar to Marcuse.

> A new political paradigm requires a new art to go along with it ...

Schoenberg

> One liberated from the conventions and clichés of the past.

Although their aesthetic tastes markedly differed (Adorno hated jazz and popular music in general), both Adorno and Marcuse supported the cause of artistic experiment, which put them at variance with orthodox Marxist thought and the Soviet theory of Socialist Realism.

Of Adorno's works, the most critical of the Marxist tradition of thought – and arguably the most influential on later developments in critical theory – is *Negative Dialectics* (1966). Here, it was argued that the notion of the dialectic as a way of resolving conflict and contradiction (a standard view that pre-dates Hegel and Marx, in Adorno's reading) was misguided.

Dialectics never completely resolves contradiction ...

The dialectical process should be considered <u>negative</u> rather than positive in quality.

What dialectics revealed, according to Adorno, was "the untruth of identity, the fact that the concept does not exhaust the thing conceived".

Against Totality – and Totalitarianism

Adorno's objective in developing his negative dialectic of "non-identity thinking" is to undermine the notion of **totality**, as well as the authority that goes with claiming to have grasped the internal workings of this. Classical Marxism certainly made such a claim, with the dialectic being treated as the key to understanding the operations of the **social totality**.

The importance of undermining any presumption of "totality" is that it sharpens our defences against totalitarian systems.

Negative dialectics very much prefigures <u>deconstruction</u>, which is similarly concerned to show that totality is an illusory notion – there are always gaps and never the full "presence" of any identity.

From such a perspective, everything is always in a state of "becoming" rather than fully-fledged "being". And when that is so, Marxism soon runs into difficulties.

Theory of the Aura

The critic and cultural theorist Walter Benjamin was a maverick figure on the fringes of the Frankfurt School. But his work shares at least some of their preconceptions. Although he died well before the School's most influential period (the later 1940s through to the 1960s), Benjamin's work nevertheless has been instrumental in helping to define what we mean by critical theory. Benjamin is perhaps best known for his theory that what marks out works of art is their "aura". This "aura" is what cannot be captured in any reproduction, as Benjamin points out in his highly influential essay, "The Work of Art in an Age of Mechanical Reproduction" (1936).

The ability to reproduce works of art mechanically, especially in quantity, is a relatively new phenomenon ...

Is my aura on straight?

It is by now a familiar phenomenon, with mass-produced prints of great artworks found in millions of households worldwide.

In Combat with Tradition

But a print of a Vincent van Gogh, no matter how high quality its reproduction, is not the real thing. In Benjamin's words, the print lacks the original's "presence in time and space, its unique existence at the place where it happens to be"; or, as he proceeds to call it, its "aura".

But there is a positive side to mechanical reproduction.

Looks like some other sort of reproduction to me...

The process emancipates the work of art from its parasitical dependence on ritual ...

... in other words, from the dead weight of <u>tradition</u> that a Rembrandt or van Gogh carries around with it.

Photography and film in particular demonstrate this emancipation. It makes no sense to ask which is the "authentic" copy in these cases. In Benjamin's view, this opens up art to the masses in a way that has never been possible before, enabling them to escape from the clutches of tradition – a highly desirable outcome for the revolutionary-minded Marxist.

Brecht's Epic Theatre

Benjamin was also one of the first champions of the German Marxist playwright Bertolt Brecht and his concept of "epic theatre". The great virtue of epic theatre for Benjamin was a clearly-defined political agenda that it self-consciously drew to the audience's attention. It "does not reproduce conditions, but, rather, reveals them", showing us the way in which the ruling classes exploit and keep us in a state of subjection to their ideology.

Through epic theatre, we come to recognize the social conditions that oppress us ...

... without being lulled into a sense of identification with "realistically" drawn characters, and thus deflected away from the recognition that revolutionary change is needed.

This is Brecht's famous "alienation effect" which permits no escapism. Epic theatre is radically political, philosophical and didactic.

It teaches the working class to question its conditions of existence, and the way in which these are portrayed in the media (by its "revelations"), and thus becomes a truly revolutionary art-form.

Russian Formalism

Although not strictly speaking a Marxist "school", the Russian Formalists were active just before and after the Soviet Revolution of 1917, and merit some consideration before moving off the topic of Marxist critical theory. Although a casualty of Stalinism and its brutally doctrinaire Socialist Realist aesthetic in 1932, Formalist ideas resurfaced in the West in the 1960s to inspire new generations of theorists in the structuralist movement. Formalist critics, such as those associated with the Moscow Linguistic Circle, concentrated their attention on literary form and literary language.

Our interests were in marked contrast to the sociologically-oriented approach of Socialist Realism enforced by Stalin's cultural commissars ...

Works of art must communicate the "correct" political message – plenty of happy workers looking to a bright Socialist future!

The Grammar of Narrative

Formalist influence can be detected in the work of such later theorists as **Roland Barthes** (1915–80), who shares the Russians' concern with "literariness" – those elements, such as the self-conscious use of literary devices, that signal that we are in the presence of "literature" as opposed to other forms of discourse.

The obsession of so many structuralist thinkers with compiling an exhaustive "grammar" of narrative has its roots in the Formalist movement.

As well as Barthes himself, we can also cite the efforts of **A.J. Greimas** (b. 1917) and **Tzvetan Todorov** (b. 1939) in this area. The practice of "narratology" in general owes much to the inspiration of Formalism.

Shklovsky's Defamiliarization

Viktor Shklovsky (1893–1984) contributed the concept of "defamiliarization" to his analysis of literary language – the "making strange" of everyday events and objects so that they appear to us in a new light.

Brecht's "alienation effect" is another version of this process which forces us to recognize, by drawing attention to stylistic devices, what lies behind actions and behaviour that we take for granted (their hidden ideological connotations). Note how both Marxism and Formalism emphasize the "hidden" elements behind the textual surface.

Bakhtin's Plural or Dialogic Meanings

Another figure from this era whose work made a belated appearance in the West was **Mikhail Bakhtin** (1895–1975). His innovative approach to literary analysis also suffered from Stalinist repression – despite his attempt to devise a Marxist philosophy of language. Bakhtin's researches on the novel strikingly prefigure poststructuralism in many ways, particularly in his insistence on the *plural quality* of meaning.

> Meaning is always contested and negotiated within society ...

> Language is "dialogic" in nature, that is, a series of encounters between individuals.

There is no fixed meaning to any narrative, therefore, and it is always open to multiple interpretation. There is a plural quality to Bakhtin's own writings, too, in that he may have published work in the 1920s under a variety of names – most notably, Valentin Voloshinov (an issue still being debated among Bakhtin commentators).

Intertextuality or Heteroglossia

Bakhtin saw novels as intensely "intertextual" – a concept further developed by the structuralist-feminist theorist Julia Kristeva. Novels are not independent unitary creations, but products that rely on "intertextuality", that is, on references to an entire complex web of past and present discourses within their culture. This process Bakhtin dubbed "heteroglossia". Heteroglossia works against the unifying tendencies within a culture, as generally advocated by the ruling establishment.

It can be considered a disruptive force aimed sharply and polemically against the official languages of its time.

Bakhtin identifies a similarly disruptive influence within the institution of the **carnival**, with its love of uncontrolled parody, whereby socio-political authority is mercilessly mocked and "made strange". The wildly satirical work of **Rabelais** (1494–1553) is for Bakhtin a prime example of this carnivalesque approach to authority (sadly lacking in the Socialist Realist enterprise).

Jakobson's Semiotic Linguistics

Roman Jakobson (1896–1982) provides a direct bridge between Russian formalist **semiotics** and later poststructuralist developments in critical theory. He began as a member of the Moscow Linguistic Circle, then, in exile, the Prague Linguistic Circle (1920), until his arrival in America (1941) where he collaborated with the seminal structuralist anthropologist **Claude Lévi-Strauss** (b. 1908).

Jakobson analysed literary aesthetics ("poetics") as a sub-branch of systematic linguistics: "The object of study in literary science is not literature but *literariness*." He means the patterns of linguistic devices that specify literary discourse.

> The addressee – or reader – is the source of aesthetic value.

	CONTEXT	
ADDRESSER	MESSAGE	ADDRESSEE
	CONTACT	
	CODE	

> Onto this map of features I superimpose corresponding functions...

	referential	
emotive	poetic	conative
	phatic	
	metalingual	

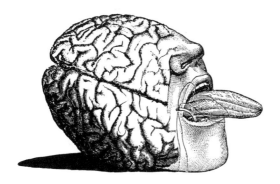

Jakobson's interest in *aphasia* (a language disorder due to brain injury) alerted him to a fundamental linguistic pattern of oppositions: **metaphor** and **metonymy**. Metaphor is a device of comparison ("strong as a lion") or imaginative unliteral description ("a glaring error"). Metonymy works by substituting an associative part for a whole ("sails" for "ships"), as follows ...

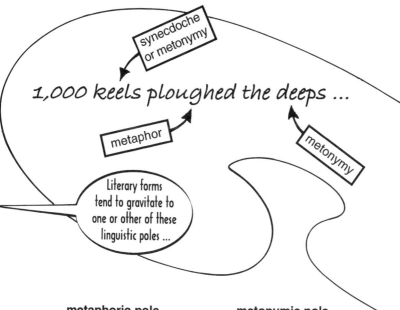

synecdoche or metonymy

1,000 keels ploughed the deeps ...

metaphor

metonymy

Literary forms tend to gravitate to one or other of these linguistic poles ...

metaphoric pole

Romantic poetry
lyrical songs
filmic metaphor
Surrealism

metonymic pole

heroic epics
Realist fiction
film montage
journalism

The Psychoanalytic Unconscious

After Marx, we can name **Sigmund Freud** (1856–1939) and his pioneering **psychoanalysis** as the next biggest influence on the evolution of critical theory. Indeed, there is a parallel between them …

I revealed an unconscious element in the economic infra-structure of society.

I discovered the unconscious in the structural economy of the individual's inner life or psyche.

SUPER-EGO
pcpt.-cs
preconscious
EGO
ID
unconscious repressed
conscious perception

Both are also **therapists**. Marx sought a cure for "economic illness" in the historical process of class struggle and revolution. Freud, circa 1900, broke away from neurological psychiatry to pursue a cure for neurotic disorders by a process of self-knowledge. For both of them, humanity's "structural defects" are real, serious but not inescapable. There is a margin of freedom to be gained by active self-knowledge.

Marxian dialectics and Freudian psychoanalysis equally emphasize a **hidden agenda** beneath our surface dimension – things are not what they seem. Critical theory follows them in attempting to tease out that agenda. Freud posits a discrepancy between our conscious "surface life" and the unconscious depth which is the unseen, unacknowledged controlling force. "Drives" at an instinctual level dictate much of what we say and do at a conscious level. Dreams, sexual abnormalities, neurotic pathologies will break through the disguises of conscious normality. Drives may be frustrated or displaced for a time – but not indefinitely.

Eventually, we have the "return of the repressed" – usually an unwelcome one!

"The return of the repressed"? Ah yes, I call that revolution!

Psychoanalysis and Critical Theory

Critical theorists have adopted the psychoanalytic idea of a "sub-text" to human activity and applied it to a variety of cultural phenomena – literature, film and media, and indeed society itself, as in the case of the Frankfurt School which married psychoanalysis to Marxism. The essential idea for critical theory is that there is nothing *accidental* in a text – in the widest sense of **text as production**. Every indication of what is hidden, repressed or displaced in its structure can be traced back to the "textual unconscious".

62

Freud himself in *The Interpretation of Dreams* (1900) suggested that Hamlet had a secret "Oedipal" desire to murder his own father (and marry his mother), hence his difficulty in taking action against the usurper Claudius. Detractors of psychoanalytic criticism object that viewing Hamlet like this is to confuse literature with reality – the "textuality of texts" is ignored in favour of "psychical analysis".

The text is treated as a window to the artist's sex-tormented soul...

– or that of his or her characters' "inner life".

Psychoanalysis does indeed owe much to literature. Freud's central dogma of the "Oedipus Complex" derives from *Oedipus Rex* by the Greek dramatist **Sophocles** (c. 496–406 BC). Psychoanalytic criticism often falls back on the analysis of fictional characterization. And Freud's classic case-studies, Little Hans, Dora, The Rat Man etc., whatever value they may have as "science", are certainly great examples of story-telling.

Structuralism and Critical Theory

We now arrive at a third influential model of the unconscious which is represented by structuralism.

Structuralism has its origin in the linguistic theory of **Ferdinand de Saussure** (1857–1913). Saussure aimed to reveal the universal structure of language as a constructed system of rules. His key idea is the relation of the **signifier** to the **signified**. The connection between the linguistic signifier c/a/t/ and the signified concept "cat" is entirely arbitrary.

The word cat has no attributes of a real "cat" but is simply the result of an agreed convention. Every language has a different signifier for this same concept or "idea" of cat.

Another Saussurean principle is that meaning in language is the product of incremental **unit differences** along a chain of signifiers:

... c / a / t / : c / u / t / : c / u / p / : p / u / p / ... etc.

What is Structuralism?

Saussure's idea of the arbitrary signifier has provoked controversy over its possible "motivation" by language-users.

Saussure's interest, however, is in language...

...as a functional system (*langue*)...

...and not as a collection of individual utterances (*parole*).

He predicted the development of what he called "semiology" – the **science of signs**...

...that would include linguistics in an overall programme of "sign-systems" analysis.

STRUCTURALISTS IN THE 1950S AND 60S PROCEEDED TO TAKE SEMIOLOGY FROM LINGUISTICS AND APPLY IT TO ALL MANNER OF SOCIAL "SIGN-SYSTEMS".

Structuralists conceive of the world as a series of interlocking sign-systems to which human beings respond in largely predictable ways ...

... as we do to traffic lights, although that's a rudimentary example.

There are far more complex sign-systems that "structure" the customs and conventions of our everyday behaviour.

Under the surface of all sign-systems is a "deep structure" – something like a genetic programme – which dictates how such systems operate. Marx located an unconscious hidden in economic production; Freud excavated it in our psychic drives. For structuralism, the unconscious is located in <u>language itself</u>. All sign-systems are analogous to language and consist of a decipherable "grammar" of rules that operate on elements of a system by conventions.

Structuralist analysis aims at revealing how we understand each other by such conventional rules - how we "signify" to each other ...

As in chess, we must play by accepted rules. These can change only by general consensus.

Let's now exemplify this by seeing how structuralism was applied to psychoanalysis. We shall look at Lacan's contribution in the 1950s and 60s.

Lacan and Structuralist Psychoanalysis

The post-Freudian <u>Jacques Lacan</u> (1901–81) famously proposed the idea that the unconscious is structured "like a language". He meant that the unconscious is only ever available to us as a "grammar system" but remains unknowable in itself.

Language exists before any one of us does. As "individuals" we are structured by what always pre-dates us as already "meaning".

This view undermines the conventional assumption of the "self" that most of us subscribe to in our everyday lives.

The self as a consistent entity enduring over time – an "inner essence" that we always suppose to be there – evaporates into the conditions of language. This is an important consequence of structuralism that has shaped postmodern critical theory.

LIKE A LANGUAGE

Lacan's Imaginary and Symbolic Realms

Lacan's work is notoriously difficult to interpret. But, as one participant in his famous series of seminars in Paris in the 1950s remarked, no matter how obscure he may be, Lacan nevertheless "produces resonances". This has proven especially the case among feminists in the late 1960s and 70s attracted to Lacan's conception of the **Imaginary** and **Symbolic** realms.

The Imaginary is the pre-self conscious state of infants up to six months, and the "mirror stage" of first self-recognition ...

The Symbolic is the social language realm that we enter at a later stage around 18 months.

The first stage is identified with the mother; the second with the father, or, in a wider sense, the "masculine" world of order and authority that we inhabit as adults. This is the Symbolic realm of pre-established language systems which in the "Name of the Father", as Lacan puts it, oppresses women.

Lacan himself was originally inspired by avant-garde **Surrealism** of the 1930s, chiefly theorized by the poet and former psychiatrist **André Breton** (1896–1966). Lacanian-inspired critics are likely to be most interested in works that self-consciously challenge the Symbolic world in some way – as Surrealism manifestly does with its reliance on dream imagery and the unconscious.

Just think of the art of <u>Salvador Dalí</u> (1904–89) and other Surrealist artists ...

BRETON

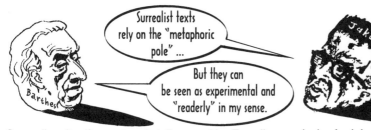

Surrealist texts rely on the "metaphoric pole" ...

But they can be seen as experimental and "readerly" in my sense.

Barthes

Jakobson

Surrealism itself was deeply influenced by Freudian analysis. And, in general, modernism's rejection of orderly "realist" styles is likely to appeal to followers of Lacan.

Barthes and the Empire of Signs

Structuralism's task of identifying the "grammar" that underlies whatever system is being studied is perhaps best exemplified (and most accessible) in the work of the cultural semiologist **Roland Barthes** (1915–80). For him, structuralism is not limited to literature and art, but can equally well apply itself to the "sign-worlds" of fashion, advertising and the media – or even wrestling, football and a restaurant menu ...

... the workings of a semiological grammar are just as fascinating in any of these systems.

Structuralism in the 1950s and 60s became a theory applicable to any and every cultural phenomenon, as Barthes shows, and little escaped its attention.

The Common Structure of Narratives

Narrative is all around us – simply an everyday fact of our world – according to Barthes. He worked out a complex method for the analysis of all possible narratives. His objective was to identify the "functional syntax" by which narrative in general is constructed.

All narrative shares a "common structure" and an "implicit system of units and rules" – a belief also held by the anthropologist Lévi-Strauss.

My researches into South American Indian myths show that these can be grouped into types – creation myths, for example.

Each particular myth functions as a "variation" on a central "theme".

Once again, we note the assumption of an unconscious "deep structure" to cultural phenomena, determining their overall form.

The Death of the Author

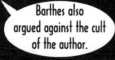

Barthes also argued against the cult of the author.

In a notorious essay of 1968, he even proclaimed the "death of the author". He meant the traditional, heroic "Author" passing on his words of wisdom to a grateful, and essentially passive, public.

I view the author instead as a channel through which language "speaks" ...

Readers are at least as much creators of narratives as authors are. "The birth of the reader must be at the cost of the death of the Author."

This has been a contentious idea. Yet, in its most basic sense, it means no more than that narratives take on a life of their own after they leave the author and pass into general circulation.

Authors cannot control the reception of their works past a certain point.

Interpretation is not something that can be legislated against with any great success – certainly not at individual level.

The Bard

This is particularly so over a period of centuries. **William Shakespeare** (1564–1616) continues to inspire widely differing – and often wildly conflicting – interpretations of his work. Shakespeare has been appropriated both by the establishment and by those in rebellion against the establishment, and no doubt will continue to be so.

Readerly versus Writerly Texts

Barthes suggests in *S/Z* (1970) that narratives can be divided into "readerly" and "writerly" categories. The latter demands the active participation of the reader; the former an attitude of passivity. Modernist novels, and indeed anything at all experimental in form – such as the novel *Tristram Shandy* (1759–67) by **Laurence Sterne** (1713–68) – are "writerly". Most 19th-century realist novels are "readerly".

I prefer writerly texts to readerly, since in the latter the author is trying to impose a particular reading on the reader ...

Whereas in experimental ones, reader participation in the creation of meaning is being openly invited.

By implication, readerly texts are authoritarian. In the rebellious climate of the 1960s, when the concept of the "death of the author" was developed, this was a grave charge to make. Critical theory since that date has had a distinctly anti-authoritarian, and often counter-cultural, edge to it.

The "Death of Man"

Structuralism also helped to promote the notion of the "death of man" (or "the subject") which has been so influential in recent critical theory. The idea here is that our traditional Enlightenment notion of "man" as the centre of cultural process – a creature able to exert domination over its environment through the exercise of reason – is a delusion. In real terms, we are controlled by **systems** ...

Language speaks through us, deep structures work through us, and we have only very limited control over our destiny.

Signifier →

← Signified

Structuralism asks us to reconsider our image of the individual, and the extent of the individual's power.

To "reconsider" is to challenge an entire cultural tradition based on a commitment to individual self-realization and self-expression (whether in the artistic or economic domains).

Intertextuality and the Symbolic Order

Semiotic theory was developed further by later poststructuralists, notably **Julia Kristeva** (b. 1941). One of her key concepts is **intertextuality**, which can simply mean that narratives are woven of echoes and traces of other texts, a web or "mosaic of quotations". Kristeva complexifies this basic semiotic idea by admixtures of Marxism, psychoanalysis and feminism. She agrees with Lacan's view of an unconscious that can never itself be "spoken", but departs from him with her idea of its continuity even after the subject enters the Symbolic order of language.

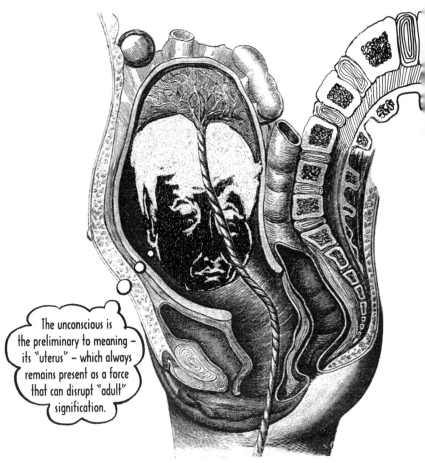

The unconscious is the preliminary to meaning – its "uterus" – which always remains present as a force that can disrupt "adult" signification.

Evidence of such "disruptions" is provided by poetry and narratives which destabilize the repressive domain of lawful Symbolic order. It is therefore also possible for Kristeva to reject the category of "essential woman" or gender as constituted by the Symbolic order.

Eco's Labyrinth

Umberto Eco (b. 1932) offers another semiotic view of intertextuality. One of the characters in his novel *The Name of the Rose* (1980) remarks that: "A book is made up of signs that speak of other signs."

Books are in dialogue with the ideas in a whole series of other books, often stretching far back into the past ...

My own semiotic theory is structured on the ideas of the "net" and the "labyrinth".

Systems are like nets. There is an infinite number of ways of traversing the distance between any two points on their surfaces. A net, for Eco, is "an unlimited territory". We might also see this as a labyrinth with no one "correct" way of journeying through it. Texts, as indeed systems as a whole, offer themselves up to multiple interpretations – "endless semiosis", as Eco says.

The success of structuralist thought in France led to a variant of Marxism called "structural Marxism", represented by its leading theorist, the philosopher **Louis Althusser** (1918–90).

It's just common sense, after all...

Ideology is a system of belief containing internal contradictions that might endanger its authority ...

Ideology requires a strategy of "force" to disguise these contradictions, if it wants to retain its power over individuals.

Ideology is therefore **disseminated** by what Althusser calls the "Ideological State Apparatuses" (institutions such as the legal system, the educational system and the media) and **maintained** by the "Repressive State Apparatus" (the police and army).

Following on from Gramsci's "hegemony" theory, Althusser also believed that ideology worked most effectively at the level of ideas – as enshrined in the Ideological State Apparatuses. The duty of the cultural critic is to identify where, and how, these ideas serve the cause of the ruling élite – as well as to identify the contradictions that reveal the gaps and flaws in the ideology in question.

Ideology "interpellates" or "hails" us, and we respond to its "signs" in reflex-like fashion, acting as they require us to do to remain captive to ideology.

Marxism can make this clear to us, so that we can escape the process of conditioning which keeps us in subjection to the dominant ideology.

Marxism is the "science of society" that enables us to see through the manipulations of the dominant ideology, and thus develop a revolutionary class consciousness.

Structuralist Marxism and Literary Criticism

The implications of Althusser's ideas were turned into critical theory by his disciple **Pierre Macherey** (b. 1939). In his book *A Theory of Literary Production* (1966), Macherey states ...

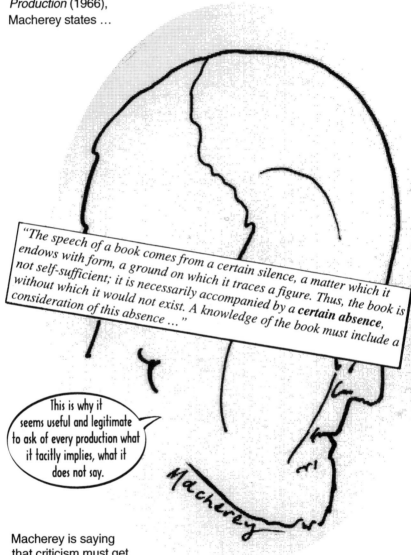

*"The speech of a book comes from a certain silence, a matter which it endows with form, a ground on which it traces a figure. Thus, the book is not self-sufficient; it is necessarily accompanied by a **certain absence**, without which it would not exist. A knowledge of the book must include a consideration of this absence ..."*

This is why it seems useful and legitimate to ask of every production what it tacitly implies, what it does not say.

Macherey is saying that criticism must get beneath the surface of a text's ideological assumptions by asking of it what it does not say. Exposing its silences and evasions is itself a **political** criticism – and, we note, an "unconscious" is once again identified.

In the critical theory of Macherey, structural Marxism becomes a "science of texts" – in effect, a sub-branch of Althusser's "science of society" – whose findings are always to be turned to political account. Literary texts have a particular ability to reveal ideological contradictions to us, which turns literary study into a politically subversive act.

What narratives disclose, when read "against the grain", are the "false resolutions" to the "real debates" that ideology constantly tries to hide from us.

In the "spontaneous ideology" of everyday life, we are generally unaware of those false resolutions. But in literature they stand out glaringly.

The novel *Jane Eyre* (1847) by **Charlotte Brontë** (1816–55) does not set out to be a discourse on the power of patriarchy, but the "madwoman in the attic" motif starkly reveals it nonetheless.

There's scary.

C. Brontë

Genetic Structuralism

A related development to structural Marxism is "genetic structuralism", the approach devised by the Franco-Romanian theorist **Lucien Goldmann** (1913–70). Genetic structuralism posits the existence of parallels – or "homologies" in Goldmann's terminology – between literary works and certain influential social groups operating at the time of those works' production.

> In my study, The Hidden God (1955), I established such parallels between the philosophy of Blaise Pascal (1623–62) and the plays of Jean Racine (1639–99) ...

GOLDMANN

> ... and the world view of the Jansenist sect that we adopted within the 17th-century Catholic Church.

Pascal

Racine

A·T
T·A
G·C
C·G
T·A
T·A
G·C
T·A
A·T
C·G

Rather than being just a reflection of the views of such groups, the greatest literature might be seen as a coherent articulation of what was otherwise "vague and confused, and contradicted by innumerable other tendencies" within the particular group in question.

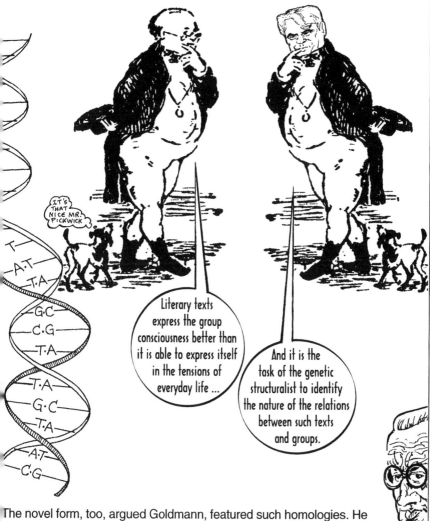

IT'S THAT NICE MR. PICKWICK

Literary texts express the group consciousness better than it is able to express itself in the tensions of everyday life ...

And it is the task of the genetic structuralist to identify the nature of the relations between such texts and groups.

The novel form, too, argued Goldmann, featured such homologies. He followed his major source of Marxist critical influence, Lukács, in tying the novel closely to the rise of bourgeois culture and the spread of the capitalist economic system.

Reader-Response Theory

Before going on to consider the reaction to structuralism in the latter decades of the 20th century, we shall take a brief sideways detour to consider another form of theory which, like Barthes', emphasized the reader's role – **reader-response**, or **reception theory** as it is sometimes called. Key figures here are the German theorist **Wolfgang Iser** (b. 1926) and the American **Stanley Fish** (b. 1938)

In both cases, the reader is given a critical role in the creation of textual meaning ...

Although Fish goes further than I do in claiming that it is the reader who actually <u>produces</u> the work of literature.

Iser assumes a greater sense of interaction between text and reader, whereby the text pushes the reader in certain directions and the reader fills in any gaps left in the text.

84

Even Fish's ostensibly more radical approach is tempered by the insistence that the reader is a member of an "interpretive community" whose shared values inform individual readings, as well as providing a criterion for assessing their validity. Reader-response or reception theory is not a particularly contentious form of critical theory.

Much of what it says about the reading process is relatively unproblematic.

Unproblematic, that is, until one delves into the complexities of the poststructuralist world ...

In that world, we can no longer take our everyday assumptions about the self, language and meaning for granted. From poststructuralism onwards, critical theory becomes much more self-consciously counter-cultural, and, let's admit it, *difficult*. Time to take the plunge ...

Poststructuralism: the Breakdown of Sign-Systems

Structuralism went too far as an all-embracing form of analysis, apparently able to explain anything and everything about human affairs and the world around us. Everything became a sign-system – in fact, nothing could *escape* being part of a sign-system.

Every constituent part can be pinned down in terms of its role within the given system's grammar ...

Increasingly, this is getting to look just too neat and even ideologically suspect.

To new generations of cultural theorists, the world was not as "orderly" as structuralism seemed to be claiming. The factor of *difference* began to exert an increasing fascination on what came to be known as the *post*structuralist movement.

86

Poststructuralism arose in the late 1960s and covers a wide range of positions. All of them are agreed that the system-building side of structuralist analysis has many critical flaws.

Systems only explain everything by frequent recourse to suppression or omission of "rogue" elements.

Whatever does not fit the system is either discarded as irrelevant or recoded to force it to fit.

To the poststructuralist mind, this was authoritarianism in action. It set out to undermine this position, introducing a note of radical scepticism into critical theory. It has been a noteworthy characteristic of critical theory, as it develops, to find authoritarianism in the methods of its immediate predecessors. Liberation from oppressive regimes, intellectual and political, is increasingly what we are being offered.

Poststructuralist Deconstruction

Arguably the most influential branch of poststructuralism, and definitely one of its most sceptic, has been **deconstruction**, as practised by its leading exponent **Jacques Derrida** (b. 1930). Derrida's early work constitutes a sustained attack on the structuralist founders – Saussure and Lévi-Strauss in particular. To his mind, structuralism is both authoritarian in manner and based on questionable philosophical premises.

Derrida argues that the standard conception of meaning in the West depends on an assumption of a "metaphysics of presence", that is, the full meaning of a word is held to be "present" to the speaker, or writer, in their mind, as they use it. He has named this assumption **logocentrism** (*logos* in Greek has the sense both of "word" and "reason").

Différance and Meaning

Such transparent presence of meaning can never be achieved, according to Derrida, because of the action of *différance*. He made up this word in French to describe the process by which meaning "slips" in the act of transmission. Words always contain within themselves traces of other meanings than their assumed primary one. It would probably be better to talk of a *field* of meaning rather than a precise one-to-one correspondence between word and meaning.

> A field that, critically enough, can never be bounded – because there is always a "surplus" of meaning at any one point.

> Given that amorphousness, <u>totalities</u> can never and <u>should never</u> form – as I had also claimed.

Bernauer Stra[ß]

45.50

In deconstruction, we move from system-building to system-dismantling. Derrida's major concern is to direct our attention to the many gaps in our systems of discourse which, try as we may, we can never quite disguise. Deconstruction is a philosophy which very self-consciously sets out to deflate philosophical pretensions about our ability to order the world.

89

Deconstructing "Binary Oppositions"

Part of Derrida's objection to structuralism is its dependence on **binary oppositions**. He considers discourse in the West in general to be founded on a series of such oppositions. One term of the binary always takes dominant priority over the other. **Man/woman** would be one such example of a "loaded" binary.

> Deconstruction aims to destabilize such binaries and the authority linked with the dominant term – hence the claims made for the theory's political implications.

white	black
true	false
good	evil
high	low
normal	abnormal

Deconstruction is no friend to the notion of hierarchy which is still deeply embedded even in the most liberal-minded of democratic societies. Feminists most certainly would agree with the notion of the man/woman binary being skewed in men's favour. Keeping it that way is what patriarchy is all about. Queer theorists are equally concerned to destabilize the binary of straight/gay, in which "straight" is taken to be the dominant term.

The Order of Things

Michel Foucault (1926–84) is another French thinker who reacted against the formal rigidity of structuralism and its insistence that everything be neatly classified in terms of its system-bound role. Foucault deepened Gramsci's inquiry into the problem of hegemony.

> My studies are concerned with the hegemonic factor of power in creating and maintaining social systems.

For him, the creation of such systems implied the marginalization and exclusion of certain vulnerable social groups in the name of "order". The fate of such groups became the central concern of Foucault's historical inquiries: the hidden agenda he was determined to bring to the surface. He delved into the "unconscious" of power.

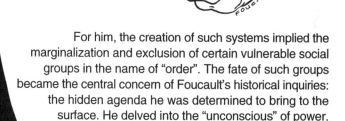

knowledge	⟶ classification
power	⟶ marginalization
order	⟶ systemized control

The Rise of Scientific Discipline

Foucault's *Madness and Civilization* (1961) describes how the mentally ill were removed to asylums that formerly housed lepers. From the 17th century onwards, this was the "Great Confinement".

Before, we had been free to roam the streets and were even granted some kind of protected status ...

Has "care in the community" reversed this process in our own day?

The objective was social control. All supposedly "deviant" behaviour became subject to strict monitoring by the ruling authorities.

Discipline and Punish (1975) traced the rise of the modern prison service; *The Birth of the Clinic* (1963) of modern medicine. In all three instances, we are witnessing the rise of "scientific" forms of social control by the authorities. The lives of individuals are to be strictly regimented.

oucault's three-volume *History of Sexuality* (1976–84) examined the rocess by which homosexuality (an unexceptionable form of sexual ehaviour in classical Greece) was gradually outlawed by Christianity, until was turned into a criminal activity.

Again, a "normative" pattern of human behaviour ad to be established in order to eradicate lifference", since that came to be regarded as a potentially <u>subversive</u> element of society.

eterosexuality became the norm (and is still largely perceived to be so to is day), with all other forms of sexual expression being treated as eviations from that norm.

Uncovering the Hidden Discourse

Foucault described his historical researches as "archaeologies" or "genealogies", designed to bring to light suppressed discourses in Western society.

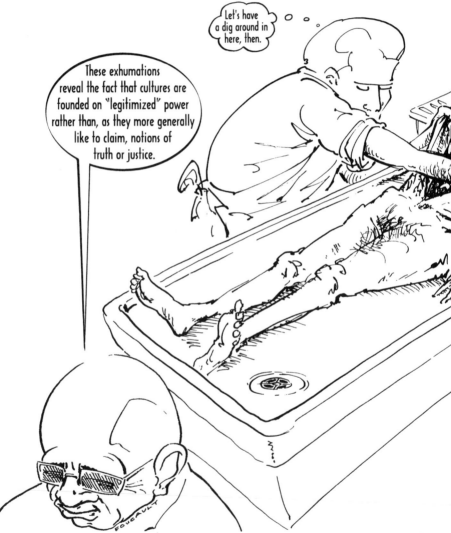

Let's have a dig around in here, then.

These exhumations reveal the fact that cultures are founded on "legitimized" power rather than, as they more generally like to claim, notions of truth or justice.

What we are studying in each case of knowledge, power and order is a particular "discourse" which, at base, is structured on power relations. As we shall see, new historicism and cultural materialism have proceeded to draw heavily on that notion.

The End of Humanism

There is no such thing as a universal "human essence" for Foucault. Behaviour, ethics, discourses and societies can – and all do – change over time. Nor is there any pattern to human history, no sense in which we are progressing – for example, to some Marxist utopia. (Foucault rejected Marxism after dabbling with it earlier on.) Indeed, Foucault regarded our conception of "man" – that is, the liberal humanist vision of the individual as the possessor of certain inalienable natural rights – as a very recent invention.

That could disappear quite easily ...

Yet another "death of man" notion to add to our list.

Foucault's vision of the human race was one that stressed *difference* rather than common elements. He continued to campaign for marginalized social groups – homosexuals, prisoners and ethnic minorities, for example – until the very end of his life.

Postmodernism is a reaction to the ideology of modernity – the belief that reason can dominate the environment around us and by so doing guarantee us material progress stretching on into the indefinite future. Modernity as a cultural phenomenon is usually traced back to the Enlightenment period in 18th-century European history, often referred to as "the Enlightenment project".

POSTMODERNISM

The Breakdown of Grand Narratives

was a "project" in the sense of actively seeking unlimited material **progress** and socio-political **liberation**. For postmodernists, modernity is a classic example of a "grand narrative" in action.

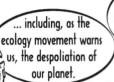

... including, as the ecology movement warns us, the despoliation of our planet.

Everyone is forced to conform to the supposed authority of the "Enlightenment project" with its commitment to progress at almost any cost ...

Again, the dislike of authority that is such a driving force in critical theory is much in evidence.

Lyotard's "Differends"

Jean-François Lyotard (1924–99) defined the postmodernist outlook as characterized by an attitude of "incredulity towards metanarratives". He meant openly expressed disbelief in the ideology or grand narrative underpinning modernity and the Enlightenment project. Modernity tended to involve the suppression of what Lyotard called "differends".

Differends are irresolvable disputes in which neither side can accept the terms of reference of the other.

For example, first nation inhabitants disputing the property claims of their territory's colonizers without surrendering their own claims in the process.

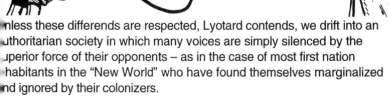

Unless these differends are respected, Lyotard contends, we drift into an authoritarian society in which many voices are simply silenced by the superior force of their opponents – as in the case of most first nation inhabitants in the "New World" who have found themselves marginalized and ignored by their colonizers.

The Postmodern Condition

Lyotard's *The Postmodern Condition* (1979) might be regarded as the bible of postmodernism as a critical theory. Its attack on grand narrative – and championship of marginalized "little narrative" – inspired a whole generation of theorists and has been instrumental in setting the agenda for the postmodern movement in general.

Narrative itself is a basic human construction. It needs no more foundation or justification than that.

Narrative only becomes problematical when it is worked up into a "grand" form that claims authoritarian or even **totalitarian** precedence over the multitude of "little" narratives (individual or small local group) that any society contains. We note here the kinship between Lyotard's idea of "differends" and the emphasis on *difference* in Derrida and Foucault. So also his idea of "constructed narrative" allies him to Barthes and other poststructuralists.

Postmodern Science

Lyotard also argued that what he called "postmodern science" (quantum mechanics, catastrophe theory and chaos theory) provides a model for us in our intellectual inquiries. Such science was "producing not the known, but the unknown" – that is, more problems than solutions, as scientists delved deeper into the bizarre world of "anti-particles", "strange attractors" and "deterministic chaos".

Quantum mechanics asserts that we cannot plot the position of any sub-atomic particle with certainty.

Chaos theory permits randomness and determinism to exist simultaneously in systems.

Complexity holds that systems "self-organize" themselves into higher levels of development.

In each case, we are confronted with counter-intuitive notions which challenge both our ordinary experience and our concept of logic.

Scientific Narrative and Relativism

There are certain scientists, the astrophysicist **John D. Barrow** (b. 1952) for example, who accept that there are unbreachable limits to our knowledge. As far as scientific inquiry is concerned, there will always, of necessity, be an...

"unknowable"-

> Any claim to be able to reach complete understanding of the nature of our universe is to be treated, therefore, with deep scepticism.

Nevertheless, we have already seen (pages 13 and 14) that...

> Lyotard's attempt to appropriate science in a "postmodern model" of critical theory enmeshed him in the controversy of the "Sokal scandal".

But, as we also noted, the question is not whether Lyotard's use of science is faulty. The issue goes deeper. Does postmodern scepticism lead to relativism that *denies* science and progress altogether?

Science for Lyotard is just another series of narratives rather than a source of truth. This is a position close to the philosopher of science Thomas Kuhn's conception of scientific "paradigms", revolutionary "shifts" in the perspectives of science that its hardline defenders would prefer to see as one uninterrupted, progressive storyline – a "grand narrative".

> Quite illicitly, grand narratives claim to <u>be</u> a source of solutions to all our socio-political problems. Marxism and science are outstanding examples of this.

> We are now encouraged to adopt a sceptical attitude towards them, with the objective of undermining their power and authority.

> We no longer have recourse to the grand narratives...

... as Lyotard proclaimed on behalf of a generation of postmodern sceptics. The idea was that institutions which were not respected could not survive indefinitely, and eventually would wither away.

The Enlightenment, "Unfinished Project"

Many critics have taken issue with this rejection of the Enlightenment project. The German philosopher **Jürgen Habermas** (b. 1929), himself a product of the Frankfurt School of critical theory, is in the forefront. For Habermas, Enlightenment ideals are still worth pursuing: modernity is an "unfinished project" which, for all its flaws, should not be jettisoned.

I deal harshly with the assumption that modernity should be regarded as an intrinsically authoritarian cultural movement, or that reason be considered our enemy.

French poststructuralist thinkers Derrida, Foucault and Lyotard come in for particular criticism from him on that score.

Habermas defends the notion of **consensus** which postmodernist theorists have turned their back on in their obsession with difference or "dissensus". The latter is politically suspect in his opinion, promoting division in our culture rather than a pragmatic approach to socio-political problems.

The Problem of Value Judgement

Poststructuralist and postmodernist critical theory sets many unresolved problems regarding value judgement. Lyotard is one of the few figures from that camp to engage with this issue in some detail. Value judgement becomes problematical in any system of thought which questions the validity of our foundations of discourse, since this tends to lead to a self-defeating relativism …

> I call for "paganism" as a way of circumventing the problems of value judgement in a postmodernist universe.

> You return to my practical work to find a method of ethics that needs no grand narrative foundation

> … if all truth is relative, then does that statement <u>itself</u> become relative in its turn?

Aristotle
(384 B.C.-
322 B.C.)

Paganism or Benthamism

Paganism demands that we make each judgement on a "case-by-case" basis with no over-arching system of rules to guide – or in any way constrain – our deliberations. "The judge worthy of his name has no true model to guide his judgements", Lyotard argues. "The true nature of the judge is to pronounce judgements, and therefore prescriptions, just so, without criteria."

Justice is not a matter of following rules but of making a judgement which circumstances <u>after the event</u> prove to have been the right one.

There are similarities to be noted here with the Utilitarian method devised by me, <u>Jeremy Bentham</u> (1748–1832).

The ethical content of an action is judged in terms of its consequences, rather than by invariant rules.

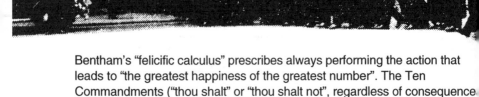

Bentham's "felicific calculus" prescribes always performing the action that leads to "the greatest happiness of the greatest number". The Ten Commandments ("thou shalt" or "thou shalt not", regardless of consequence or happiness) are *out*.

Seductive though the idea of treating every case on its merits can be, the obvious problem with such a system is that it seems to leave us at the mercy of a judge's individual whims (which the Ten Commandments do not).

To operate on a "case-by-case" model is to put more faith in the Rousseau-like "basic goodness" of human nature than history gives us cause to.

Humans are born naturally good but are corrupted by the false values of society.

The whole issue of value judgement is the Achilles heel of the poststructuralist–postmodernist movement.

Rousseau

The desire to undermine institutional authority, and its assumed authoritarianism, very quickly runs into such objections and charges of arbitrariness, although one can appreciate the general ideal that drives the desire.

Postmodernism in the Service of Capitalism

Shouldn't that be 'Surrealism at the service of the Revolution'?

Fredric Jameson (b. 1934) argues that postmodernism's swing away from generalizing "grand narrative" theory serves the cause of capitalism. For Jameson, postmodernism is less a theory in its own right than a symptom of our current cultural impasse, in which all opposition to capitalism is being systematically eradicated.

Postmodernism is not the cultural dominant of a wholly new social order, but a consequence of yet another <u>systemic modification</u> of capitalism itself.

Late capitalism has invested heavily in new digital technologies, and claims that these have created a new kind of "postmodern" society.

The old order's commitment to competing grand narratives – socialism versus capitalism, for example – can now be discarded. As Jameson points out, this simply leaves us defenceless against the power of global capitalism. Jameson still believes that the Marxist analysis of history is the correct one, and that a "new international proletariat" will eventually emerge to overcome late capitalism and its postmodern theories.

My refusal to adopt a set system of belief...

...can also be seen at work in my concept of the "event".

Existence is a series of discrete events for me.

There is no underlying pattern or purpose to existence ...

We should respond to each event...

...as it occurs...

...as creatively as possible,

...without preconceptions.

SORRY... WRONG SORT OF LYOTARD

What we should reject is any scheme such as the Marxist –

...with its inbuilt Hegelian totalitarian system of history –

...which **does** see a pattern to human affairs leading to "inevitable" revolutions and proletarian utopias.

107

Techno-science and the Inhuman

In Lyotard's view, the future is always "open". He is deeply opposed to all attempts to foreclose this openness in any way. The "openness" in Derrida's "deconstructionist" criticism is very similar in this respect. Hence Lyotard's break with Marxism, and hence also his criticism in later life of the forces of "techno-science", the new technology as appropriated by the multinationals.

Multinational techno-science aims to substitute computers for human beings wherever possible, in orde to exert as much control over the environment as it can.

Lyotard dubbed thi process a mov towards "th inhuman". He calle on humanity to resis this latest attempt t eliminate **differenc** from the worl Computers – unlik human beings – ar entirely predictabl and controllable and not much give to revolution again the authorities eithe

Strangely enough, however, certain feminist theorists – most notably **Donna Haraway** (b. 1944) and **Sadie Plant** (b. 1964) – have welcomed the new technology as a means of redrawing the gender map and breaking the pattern of male superiority in our culture.

Haraway

Plant

A Feminist Response to the Inhuman

To combine with technology is, for such theorists, to escape male control.

I see the Internet as a female-friendly space to be turned to feminist advantage.

I make the case for women turning themselves into "cyborgs" – creatures part human and part machine.

Plant

Where I see the threat of the inhuman, they see the possibility of liberation from biological constraints.

I'd rather be a cyborg than a goddess", as Haraway provocatively declares. Some critics from within the feminist movement have been just as unhappy as Lyotard about such a move away from the realm of the human. One might see a "new humanism" developing at such points, to replace the old discredited one with its emphasis on competitive individualism.

109

The Sociology of Seduction

In a move similar to Lyotard's, French sociologist **Jean Baudrillard** (b. 1929) encourages us to use "seduction" on systems as a method of undermining their "masculinist" assumption of authority.

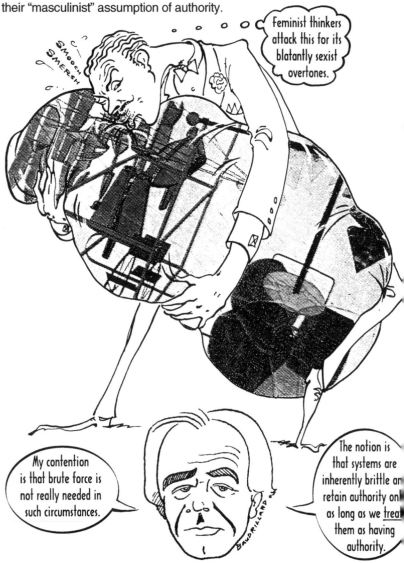

Feminist thinkers attack this for its blatantly sexist overtones.

My contention is that brute force is not really needed in such circumstances.

The notion is that systems are inherently brittle and retain authority only as long as we treat them as having authority.

Once *you* lose your fear of systems, *they* lose any hold they had over you. systems can be "beguiled". It would be nice if it were that simple, although practice it rarely is. One wonders how one would go about "beguiling" the police force!

Against the Marxist Fetishism of Production

Baudrillard's work has been just as harsh as Lyotard's on the grand narratives of our time. Marxism is dismissed, for example, for having an obsession with production that rivals that of capitalism at its worst.

A spectre haunts the revolutionary imagination – the phantom of production.

Baudrillard's mocking words are guaranteed to raise the blood pressure of the average orthodox Marxist.

Whereas I argue for continued involvement in politics at a "little" narrative level, Baudrillard becomes steadily more nihilistic and apolitical as his career progresses.

A World of Hyperreal Simulacra

Baudrillard contends that we now inhabit a world of **hyperreal simulacra**.

He is notorious for having implied that the Gulf War of 1991 was a <u>simulation</u> for television ...

Of course, the Gulf War <u>never happened</u>. I mean that nothing at all – no deeper or hidden meaning – lies behind signs any more.

He is attracted instead to "signs without referents, empty, senseless, absu and elliptical signs". The future is not so much open here, one might say, a *empty*.

Disneyworld America

To seek out "signs without referents" is to reject discourses such as Marxism and to render value judgements, political as well as aesthetic, more or less pointless. That does seem to be the message coming out of Baudrillard's later work. Value judgement is criticized in his study *America* (1986) as an essentially European preoccupation that belongs to the past.

Any nostalgia we feel for this is misplaced. The attraction of America is that it has left such considerations behind.

Postmodern America has gone *beyond* meaning into the realm of the "hyperreal". Baudrillard even speaks of the desirability of the "extermination of meaning" by means of "theoretical violence" – which certainly brings the nihilism of his thought to the fore. Unless, of course, his rhetorical exaggerations are meant to provoke our reactions.

When Did Postmodernism Begin?

Postmodernism has also drawn extensively on the work of the American architectural theorist **Charles Jencks** (b. 1939), who provocatively argued that modernism died at the precise time that an award-winning example of modernist architecture, the Pruitt-Igoe housing complex in St Louis, Missouri (a fairly typical "new brutalist" project of tower blocks), was demolished.

Of course, this drawing is a symbolic representation of this brutal architec– Urrk!!!

The time being 3.32 pm, 15 July 1972 ...

Jencks

114

The Double-Coding of Postmodernism

Jencks is a notable critic of this modernist new brutalism who claims that architecture should be able to work on several levels simultaneously, appealing to the general public no less than to the architectural profession.

I championed the idea of "double coding" whereby architects engage in a dialogue with the past. Their buildings regain some familiar features from past styles for the public to latch onto.

The aim was to satisfy both one's peers and the public by mixing together past and present styles in a synthetic fashion. That has since become a very widespread architectural practice, as a glance around almost any Western city today will readily reveal.

Postmodern Pastiche and Irony

Much of postmodernist art and literature has adopted Jencks's principle of double coding. The idea is to "mix-and-match" familiar forms in deliberate *pastiche* quotation rather than experiment formally in the manner of the modernist movement. Painters have gone back to representational art, authors to "realist"-style novels – often consciously imitating the linguistic register of the past, as in the novels of **Peter Ackroyd** (b. 1949).

The requirement is that one does so with a certain amount of <u>irony</u> which acknowledges the difference between the cultural contexts of the past and the present.

Even in the realm of postmodern theory we can see such principles at work. The new historicists – coming shortly – try to establish a sense of dialogue with older forms of historicist thought.

Anti-Oedipus and Schizoanalysis

On the wilder shores of postmodernism we find **Gilles Deleuze** (1925–95) and **Felix Guattari** (1930–92), whose *Anti-Oedipus* (1972) is an attack on the concept of authority in general and the allegedly authoritarian theories of Marxism and Freudianism in particular. Psychoanalysis for them is a repressive system which forces individuals to conform to restrictive social norms of behaviour. Deleuze and Guattari put their faith instead in "schizoanalysis".

> The schizophrenic provides a model for resistance to authority.

> Unlike Freud's "model neurotic", the schizophrenic refuses to be forced into adopting a consistent social identity.

> Far better to be multiple personalities than a single dysfunctional one.

Deleuze

Guattari

"Oedipus" becomes Deleuze and Guattari's shorthand name for the complex of social and institutional pressures by which psychoanalysis tries to make us conform and repress our desires. Neither Freud nor Lacan comes out of this exercise particularly well.

> Daft I call it.

Anti-Oedipal Networks of Communication

In *Anti-Oedipus* and its sequel, *A Thousand Plateaus* (1980), Deleuze and Guattari unleash a series of strange concepts designed to undermine our standard world-view – "desiring machines", "bodies without organs", "rhizomes" and "nomadic thought", for example.

All of us are desiring machines but find our desire being curbed by "Oedipus" at almost every step of the way.

Desiring machines are driven by libidinal energy and are therefore perceived by the authorities – such as those in control of Oedipus – to be a threat to social order.

"Bodies without organs" are part of the process by which desire is repressed. Capital, for instance, constitutes the body without organs of capitalism: that is, its sterile and unproductive component.

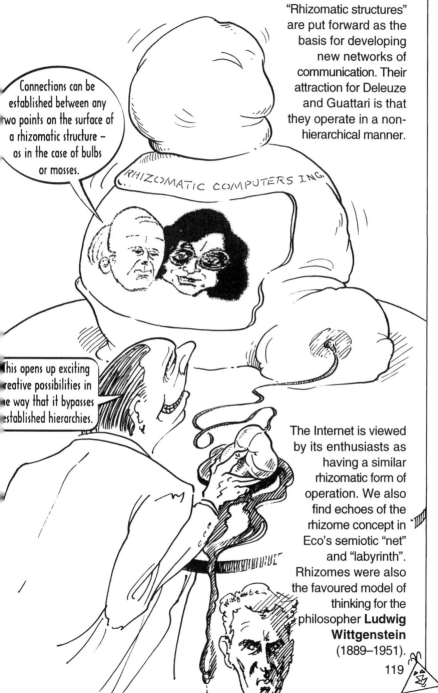

"Rhizomatic structures" are put forward as the basis for developing new networks of communication. Their attraction for Deleuze and Guattari is that they operate in a non-hierarchical manner.

Connections can be established between any two points on the surface of a rhizomatic structure – as in the case of bulbs or mosses.

This opens up exciting creative possibilities in the way that it bypasses established hierarchies.

The Internet is viewed by its enthusiasts as having a similar rhizomatic form of operation. We also find echoes of the rhizome concept in Eco's semiotic "net" and "labyrinth". Rhizomes were also the favoured model of thinking for the philosopher **Ludwig Wittgenstein** (1889–1951).

"Nomadic thought" becomes the ideal for Deleuze and Guattari. It is tied to no particular system or source of authority. Authority for them is inherently territorial and thus is the enemy of desire, which does not respect the concept of boundaries.

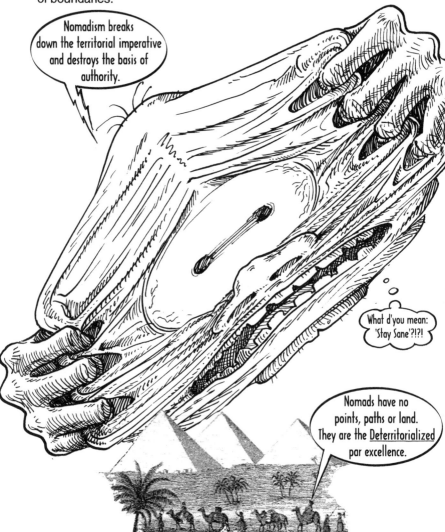

Nomadism breaks down the territorial imperative and destroys the basis of authority.

What d'you mean: 'Stay Sane'?!?!

Nomads have no points, paths or land. They are the <u>Deterritorialized</u> par excellence.

Which is to say that nomads simply ignore authority – much in the way that Lyotard is exhorting us to do in *The Postmodern Condition* by ceasing to pay any attention to fixed grand narrative territories.

Post-Marxism: The Breakdown of Marxism

By the later 20th century, Marxism began to lose support in the West. The brutal legacy of Communist tyranny in the Eastern bloc and Asia constituted an increasing source of embarrassment to the Western left. A position known as "post-Marxism" was gradually developed. In practice, it involved a rejection of most of the tenets of orthodox Marxism …

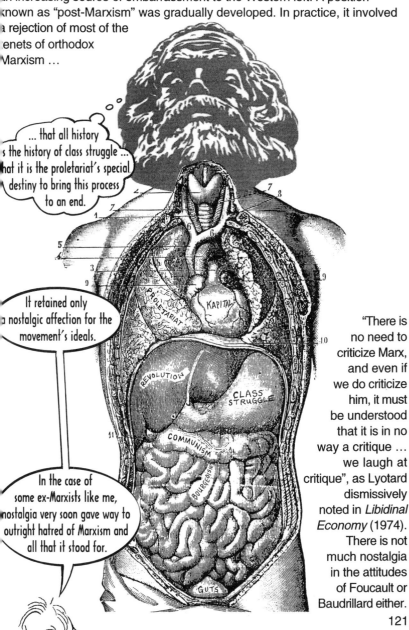

… that all history is the history of class struggle … that it is the proletariat's special destiny to bring this process to an end.

It retained only a nostalgic affection for the movement's ideals.

In the case of some ex-Marxists like me, nostalgia very soon gave way to outright hatred of Marxism and all that it stood for.

"There is no need to criticize Marx, and even if we do criticize him, it must be understood that it is in no way a critique … we laugh at critique", as Lyotard dismissively noted in *Libidinal Economy* (1974). There is not much nostalgia in the attitudes of Foucault or Baudrillard either.

A Post-Marxist Answer to Capitalism

Post-Marxist theorists such as **Ernesto Laclau** (b. 1935) and **Chantal Mouffe** (b. 1943), on the other hand, deliberately draw on a wide range of poststructuralist, postmodernist and feminist thought to attack the evils of capitalist society. They adopt a very pragmatic attitude towards the construction of a new theoretical synthesis that builds on the liberationist ideals of Marxism.

New social movements around the globe – ecological, ethnic, sexual, feminist – indicate that Marxism has been bypassed.

Its message is no longer relevant to rapidly changing socio-political circumstances.

A fresh approach was desperately needed if the onward march of capitalism was to be countered at all.

Laclau and Mouffe's controversial study *Hegemony and Socialist Strategy* (1985) constituted a rallying cry on behalf of these new social movements, more worthy of support by the left than the out-of-date socialist programme of orthodox Marxism committed to centralized parties and trades unions.

Something much more flexible is needed in the new cultural climate of the later 20th century ...

A "radical democratic politics" freed from the sterile debates of "old left" politics.

The Failures of Marxian Theory

Laclau and Mouffe particularly took issue with the Gramscian concept of hegemony. This was little more than an admission of defeat in the face of some highly problematical gaps in Marxist theory. Hegemony attempts to explain why Marx's predications were taking far longer to come about than his theory had prescribed.

It'll happen if you wait long enough...

To us, this is a case of special pleading ...

An ad hoc revision designed to protect the theory's authority in the face of persistent failure for a century or more.

There was something obviously lacking in the theory *itself* that led to its failure to predict accurately.

There were flaws in Marxism's concepts of class and class consciousness, for example, that rendered it ineffective in cultural analysis. There was also a general failure to recognize that the world had altered in such a way as to undermine many of Marxism's most cherished beliefs.

As Marcuse and many earlier theorists had already pointed out ...

...still waiting...

The working class no longer exists in anything like its traditional form. It cannot be counted on to lead the way in the overthrow of capitalism.

To quote the title of a controversial book by one such theorist, **André Gorz** (b. 1924), it was a case of *Farewell to the Working Class* (1980).

Beyond Doctrinaire Marxism

Post-Marxists in general reject the doctrinaire quality of orthodox Marxism which demands unswerving unity of thought and belief – as symbolized by the Communist Party – and almost pathological dislike of spontaneity and individualism. The call is for a much more pragmatic approach to cultural problems, free of the preconceptions of orthodox Marxist thought which refuses to countenance any tinkering with its basic philosophical categories.

The working class has ceased to exist in its 19th-century form.

It is now so diffuse in a post-industrial age as to lack any coherent identity and revolutionary potential.

I am all **too** familiar with designer sportswear...

Such ideas, floated by many post-Marxist thinkers, have outraged doctrinaire Marxists. Post-Marxists, on the other hand, want to retain the spirit of Marxism without any of its messy history of failure (to most of them) or authoritarian bias.

The Spectre of Marx

A particularly pertinent example of that attempt – to retain the spirit without the discredited content of Marxist thought – can be found in Derrida's *Spectres of Marx* (1993).

Marx has himself become a "spectre" we cannot expel from our consciousness or our culture. His legacy continues to hold important lessons for us. Derrida argues that there will be "no future without Marx".

There is still widespread and <u>increasing</u> economic exploitation in the world – but no indication that this is about to stop.

The multinationals are very much in control. Political oppression is still rife too. Its continued existence calls for principled resistance from the left, just as it did in Marx's day.

A Plural Marx

But Derrida's Marx is, as he puts it, "plural".

Marx was the first himself to say that his philosophy would be *shed* by changing historical circumstances. He is therefore *as a thinker* open to multiple interpretation and not some set body of doctrine to be followed blindly by acolytes no matter what the political situation.

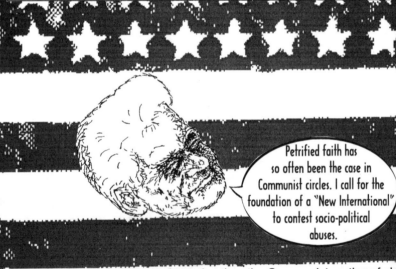

Petrified faith has so often been the case in Communist circles. I call for the foundation of a "New International" to contest socio-political abuses.

But this is to be a much looser formation than the Communist parties of old. Derrida dismisses all the works of the Party "dogma machine" for having distorted Marx's original message of **liberation**.

The "End of History"

Derrida is particularly concerned in *Spectres of Marx* to refute the notion – current in the early 1990s, in the aftermath of the collapse of the Soviet Union and its empire – that liberal democracy had finally triumphed over all other forms of government.

We have witnessed the end of history.

Foo Koo Yah Man

This is supposed to confirm an "end" to the history of ideological conflict between left and right – the forces of change and the forces of reaction – that marked the last few centuries in Europe. <u>As if</u> this history has been <u>resolved</u> ...

The American political scientist **Francis Fukuyama** (b. 1952) even wrote a book called *The End of History* (1992) in support of this claim. To Derrida, this amounted to ideological disinformation. The "spectre" of Marx will continue to haunt us, Derrida insists, no matter what the ideologues of liberal democracy might think. Even if we wanted to, we could not simply eradicate him from our consciousness – and we should not want to, anyway.

Our Complicity in Ideology

One of the most thought-provoking figures in post-Marxism is the Slovenian cultural critic **Slavoj Žižek** (b. 1949). He challenges the assumption that ideology is a "conspiracy" by counter-proposing that we are all as individuals *complicit* in the operation of ideology. Žižek's idea is that we are well aware of the gaps and contradictions in our ideology. We just turn a blind eye to them most of the time.

Ideology succeeds – not because it "interpellates" us to do its bidding like robots – but because we *want* it to succeed.

We *want* to believe that we live under a consistent system of belief, and, in effect, we *interpellate ourselves* to make it seem so.

So, contrary to the views of Althusser and Gramsci, the "system" only works because we pretend to ourselves that it does. *We* fill in the gaps and disguise the contradictions, not some political élite on our behalf.

If we all work together...

...we can totally disrupt the system.

Žižek

Once we realize we are doing that, of course, it becomes all the easier to call the system into question and institute radical change.

Rather like Lyotard, it becomes a case of withdrawing one's support and waiting – or at least hoping – for the system to collapse. Again, it would be nice if it really were that simple. Žižek's criticism does at least have the merit of "empowering" ordinary people who are otherwise seen as helplessly in the control of a political élite.

The New Historicism

Poststructuralism and postmodernism are essentially anti-historicist theories. They deny the existence of any "grand" pattern to history regarded as a steady progress towards some distant goal. But there was a return of sorts to historicist thought in the latter decades of the 20th century which took the form of "new historicism".

There _is_ a sense of dialogue with the past here – in the tradition of "double coding" – but this new brand of historicism is still very different from the old.

New historicism often takes much of its lead from the thought of figures such as Foucault.

Historical periods are treated as power struggles that leave their "imprint" on all the artistic production of their time. There is an echo of Marxist "reflection theory" here, discussed earlier, although of a much more sophisticated variety than Plekhanov's crudely materialistic one.

The leading American new historicist critic **Stephen Greenblatt** (b. 1937), with his books *Renaissance Self-Fashioning* (1980) and *Shakespearean Negotiations* (1988), influenced the development of critical theory in the Anglo-American world. Greenblatt's work on Renaissance literature emphasizes that such material is caught up in the power struggles of its time.

Shakespeare's plays, for instance, bear the mark of those struggles, rather than offering us any unequivocal message about the "human condition" that transcends their time.

These plays are to be considered instead "places of dissension" where competing ideological narratives are in conflict.

Greenblatt

A much-imitated aspect of Greenblatt's analytical method is the juxtaposition of literary and non-literary texts in order to expose the power struggles of the time: a police report alongside a Shakespeare play, for example.

Cultural Materialism

Cultural materialism is closely related to new historicism in style and method, and is perhaps best seen in the work of the English critics **Alan Sinfield** (b. 1941) and **Jonathan Dollimore** (b. 1948).

We operate on the basic premise that "culture is political", and build on the original formulation of that term by the cultural theorist <u>Raymond Williams</u> (1921–88) ...

"Culture" as the analysis of all forms of signification ... within the actual means and conditions of their production.

Both Sinfield and Dollimore have also been very active in Shakespeare studies. They argue strongly for a politicized reading of the plays, as opposed to the more conservative notion of Shakespeare as a universal genius far above the mere concerns of ideology (still a very prevalent notion in Britain).

134

A Politicized Shakespeare

Foucault is a clear source of influence in such studies.

Shakespeare's plays are analysed in terms of their place in the discourses of power at their time of writing.

Power becomes the hidden agenda that the critic is concerned to bring to the audience's attention.

"Political Shakespeare" has become a very controversial notion that has ruffled many feathers in Renaissance studies ...

... and the adversarial quality of recent cultural theory is made very evident.

The Theory of Postcolonialism

The American-Palestinian critic **Edward Said**'s (b. 1935) *Orientalism* (1978) gave impetus to the development of postcolonialism as a significant area of critical theory in its own right. His study examined the way in which the Orient – in this case, what we now call the "Middle East" – came to be constructed in Western culture as a mysterious "other" onto which the West projected its fantasies, sexual and otherwise.

The Orient is a fiction that only serves to represent the hidden desires of Western culture ...

Golly-exotic totty!

It's made to look erotic, exotic and exciting.

This is an area "beyond", where normal Western morality and rationality cease to apply. A desire for decadence can be indulged. But there is also something to be feared in this "uncontrolled" area.

The West has deliberately "infantilized" the East. It has done so not only ideologically but as an excuse precisely to exert political control over the East. "Orientalism is a Western style for dominating, restructuring and having authority over the Orient."

From the 18th century onwards, Western literature and art is complicit in this programme of colonial subjection.

Any criticism which is to address this phenomenon must be clearly politically motivated.

A Palestinian himself, Said has been a leading voice in the movement for Palestinian self-determination, and a severe critic of Israeli state policy towards the Palestinian people.

Fanon's Anti-Colonialism

Said has drawn on the pioneer work of the psychiatrist and political theorist **Frantz Fanon** (1925–61). Fanon's *Black Skin, White Masks* (1952) explored the ways in which the black colonized races internalized the ideas of their white colonizers.

I have observed how those "introjected" ideas will lead the colonized victim to regard their own blackness as having almost entirely negative associations.

Fanon's *Wretched of the Earth* (1961) uncompromisingly defends violence in the cause of overthrowing colonialism. The revolution in Algeria against the French in the 1950s and 60s became exemplary of what was needed. Fanon was an active member of the Algerian Liberation Front (FLN) at the time.

Poststructuralist Hybridity

More recently, the work of **Homi K. Bhabha** (b. 1949) has also had considerable influence on postcolonial debates.

One of his key ideas is "hybridity" ...

... the transformational value of change lies in the rearticulation, or translation, of elements that are <u>neither the One</u> (unitary working class) <u>nor the Other</u> (the politics of gender) <u>but something else besides</u>, which contests the terms and territories of both.

Bhabha

That notion of "*something else besides*", with its anti-essentialist overtones, indicates the poststructuralist influences on Bhabha's thought.

Subaltern Studies

Gayatri Chakravorty Spivak (b. 1941) is a leading member of the Subaltern Studies group at Delhi University. She is best known for having introduced poststructuralist theories – especially Derrida's deconstruction – into postcolonial debate.

> I do so in the cause of feminism, exploring the way Indian women have occupied a "subaltern" position ...

> ... which means we are oppressed <u>both</u> by traditional notions of patriarchy and by colonialism.

As one of Spivak's essays puts it, "Can the subaltern speak?" The concept "subaltern" was first defined by Gramsci in 1934; the New Delhi group use it for the Indian peasantry *doubly* oppressed, first by colonialism then by India's own political élite.

Theory as Sexual Politics

FEMINISM

Feminism has exerted enormous influence on critical theory.

...has demonstrated well-honed ability to absorb what it wants from a whole range of other theories – Marxism, deconstruction, postmodernism, etc. – while still pursuing a clearly-defined agenda of its own.

What's on our agenda? Such concerns as the nature and mechanisms of male oppression ...

As well as the nature of female experience under these mechanisms.

And, in critical terms, the challenge that can be created to male domination in areas such as the arts by the construction of a female "canon" of works.

141

A Feminist Literary Canon

Literary "canons" of Great Works have generally been weighted in the past towards male figures. Feminism's challenge has led to the recovery and subsequent republication – often for the first time since the original edition – of a series of novels by hitherto neglected female authors of the 18th and 19th centuries. Two such works of recovery are **Dale Spender**'s (b. 1943) *Mothers of the Novel: 100 Good Women Novelists before Jane Austen* (1986) and **Elaine Showalter**'s (b. 1941) *A Literature of their Own: British Women Novelists from Brontë to Lessing* (1977).

Feminism and Marxism

So-called "second wave" feminism from the 1960s and 70s onwards has adopted a significantly more militant stance towards patriarchy than the "first wave" did. Such militancy has often involved heavy criticism of Marxism, held to be in league with patriarchy, if only unwittingly. The American feminist **Heidi Hartmann** (b. 1945) famously spoke of "the unhappy marriage between Marxism and feminism".

Although Hartmann was still hoping that an accommodation could be reached, somehow or other, Marxism having its positive points, several of her contemporaries act as if the divorce has already taken place – and not before time!

Post-Marxist Feminism

Marxist feminists themselves have become increasingly critical of Marxism in the last few decades, and, while acknowledging the theory's scope and power, have come to regard it as a bastion of patriarchal attitudes holding back the cause of women.

Feminist thought now generally has a "post-Marxist" bias. It is no longer willing to wait until the "revolution" comes about for gender issues to be addressed seriously. Some feminists have even gone so far as to argue that the revolution is unlikely to happen at all *unless* gender issues are resolved first.

144

The Theory of Gynocriticism

Among the significant theorists of second-wave Anglo-American feminism, as far as the development of critical theory is concerned, we might instance Elaine Showalter, **Kate Millett** (b. 1934), the team of **Sandra Gilbert** (b. 1936) and **Susan Gubar** (b. 1944), and **Ellen Moers** (b. 1928).

Showalter coined the term "gynocritics" to describe what she thought feminists ought to be doing in their reading of literature ...

"Gynotexts" should be the subject of our attention – narratives which deal specifically with women's experience.

The main concern of the gynocritic is to trace "the evolution or laws of a female literary tradition". The clear intention is to revise cultural history such that women are brought in from the *margins of discourse* where patriarchy historically has tended to banish them.

145

Against Patriarchy

Kate Millett's *Sexual Politics* (1970) had considerable impact on the development of second-wave feminist thought. Her denunciation of Freud sparked off an intense debate about his influence on patriarchy.

Sometimes the sword mightier than the 'pen is'...

Gasp!

His concept of "penis envy" is proof of Freud's masculinist bias ...

But there is also a substantial body of support for Freud from within feminist circles.

The work of **Juliet Mitchell** (b. 1940), *Psychoanalysis and Feminism* (1974), is a particularly notable "return to Freud" from a critical theory perspective.

reud remains something of a battleground in feminist theory. It is still very
uch a live issue whether he furthers or retards the cause of women. Millett
so emphasized the patriarchalist role played in literature by such novelists
s **D.H. Lawrence** (1885–1930) and **Norman Mailer** (b. 1923).

iterature has in fact become one of the prime sites of second wave feminist
search, and the representation of women one of its key concerns.

The Surplus Woman

The team of Gilbert and Gubar's *The Madwoman in the Attic* (1979) takes as an image of "subordinate woman" the "case-history" of Bertha Rochester in Charlotte Brontë's novel *Jane Eyre* (1847). She is symbolic of women's vulnerability in a patriarchal society: a vulnerability felt no less by female authors than by their readers.

If women become <u>surplus</u> to male requirements, they are simply hidden away, as "madwoman" Bertha Rochester was by her husband.

Often such women are classified as "hysteric" in order to justify their maltreatment.

The madwoman in the attic comes to stand for female experience in general under the dominion of male power.

Against the Male Canon

Ellen Moers's study *Literary Women* (1978) is also representative of the growing desire in Anglo-American feminism to construct a canon around women authors. Her concern – as with Showalter and Spender – is to establish a specifically female literary tradition that breaks the male stranglehold on the canon.

The dean of American critics Harold Bloom recently published his <u>Western Canon</u> (1994) – and, yes, there are a few women in it, but only those already "canonized" by male academics ...

Of course this is a concern because the essentially <u>male canon</u> still forms the basis for most degrees in English literature.

The tradition that Moers and others seek is one that recognizably deals with key aspects of female experience over the past few centuries – such as childbirth and economic dependence on men.

"Heroinism" in Women's Literature

Moers's interest lies in "literary feminism", or as she memorably dubs it, "heroinism". Heroinism is the woman writer setting out "to create a heroic structure for the female voice in literature". The phenomenon is datable from the late 18th and early 19th centuries.

I identify authors such as <u>Mary Wollstonecraft</u> (1759–97) as instrumental in its development.

Gothic literature was a genre of the time in which women were notably active, both as authors and readers.

"Gothik" is an example of what Moers calls "traveling heroinism", or the "female picaresque", which allowed women characters to be tested outside the domestic sphere and its lack of "adventure". A capability for moral development was demonstrated by women that perhaps even outstripped that of men.

French Feminism: *écriture féminine*

French feminism is noticeably more theory-orientated than the Anglo-American. It is particularly concerned with the factor of "**difference**", which carries Derrida's hallmark. The concept of *écriture féminine* offers a direct challenge to the assumptions of patriarchy. The battleground in this case is language. For **Hélène Cixous** (b. 1937), *écriture féminine* constitutes a form of writing which enables women to present themselves as *they* want, rather than as men want them to be.

> Woman must write herself, must write about women and bring women to writing ...

> Woman must write woman. And man, man.

The differences between the sexes are such, it would seem, that they can hardly talk to each other any more. Cixous does allow that certain male writers – **Jean Genet** (1910–86) most notably – may aspire to the condition of *écriture féminine*.

151

The Undecidable of *écriture féminine*

A difficulty with Cixous's conception of <u>écriture féminine</u> is the sheer vagueness of the term itself.

It is impossible to define a feminine practice of writing, for this practice can never be <u>theorized</u>.

Mais oui...

My friend Cixous is trading on the term "undecidability", a consequence of the deconstructionist criticism of <u>logocentrism</u>.

Deciding what does, and what does not, come under the heading of *écriture féminine* therefore becomes a considerable challenge to authoritarian boundaries. "Difference feminists" seem to appreciate the freedom of manoeuvre that such vagueness creates.

Does Difference Lead to Separatism?

Luce Irigaray (b. 1932) has been a particular proponent of difference feminism. Women's identity is for Irigaray, unlike men's, very diffuse.

> It is useless, then, to trap women in the exact definition of what they mean. And the same goes for <u>écriture féminine</u>.

> <u>Écriture féminine</u> is designed to capture this diffuseness and difference.

> This emphasis on difference leaves Irigaray vulnerable to the charge of biological essentialism.

> The trouble with biological essentialism is that it denies the possibility of meaningful change. Men and women are trapped by their respective biological make-up.

The most logical conclusion to such a belief is **separatism** from men, which did indeed become a very powerful movement within feminism in the last decades of the 20th century (with Irigaray being one of its most vocal champions), although its influence is of late on the wane.

Two Champions of Modern Feminism

A classic pioneering work, *The Second Sex* (1949) by **Simone de Beauvoir** (1908–86), set much of the agenda for modern feminism. Existentialism and Marxism combine in her challenge to society which demands "feminine" behaviour from women and "constructs" them in opposition to men as the assumed dominant sex. There is no biological or psychological necessity for this. Becoming a woman means being indoctrinated into a certain code of behaviour that can be resisted.

Germaine Greer (b. 1939) is one of many "second wave" feminists inspire by Beauvoir. Greer's book *The Female Eunuch* (1970) detailed how wome are schooled into constructing their bodies as objects of male desire.

Some feminists, for instance **Rosalind Coward**, complain of what they call "womanism": the assumption that the female perspective is by definition the only correct one, and thus completely beyond any possible criticism.

> The anti-womanist argument is a plea for a more <u>inclusive</u> feminism that does not simply discount the male perspective altogether.

Coward

> Similar arguments against biological essentialism can be found in the work of Julia Kristeva.

> I accuse difference feminism of having allowed itself to sink into an essentialist cult of <u>Woman</u>, whereas I want it to speak for both sexes.

Postfeminism and Positive Womanhood

We can now even speak of **postfeminism**. It stands in relation to feminism much in the way that post-Marxism does to Marxism. The attack on womanism might be seen as an instance of this phenomenon in action.

Postfeminism represents a move away from the culture of victimhood that has so often been cultivated by second-wave feminism ...

We must pass on from woman as "victim" of patriarchy, male sexuality, etc., towards a more positive image of woman seen to have the capability to choose from a range of lifestyles.

A Parallel with Post-Marxism

Although it is at best a loose term, postfeminism represents something of a backlash against the more doctrinaire forms of feminist thought. But it has been attacked in its turn for being anti-feminist. **Tania Modleski** (b. 1949), for example, has accused postfeminists of "negating the critiques and undermining the goals of feminism – in effect delivering us back to a prefeminist world".

Again, there are parallels to be drawn between such debates and those between Marxists and post-Marxists.

In both, accusations of "aiding the enemy" are all too common.

Postfeminism might also be brought under the heading of postmodernism.

The critique of orthodox feminist thought constitutes yet another rejection of "grand narrative" – in this instance, of second-wave feminism with its essentialist bias and separatist sympathies. Postfeminists share the tendency of their post-Marxist, postmodernist and poststructuralist counterparts to view their predecessors as **authoritarian**.

QUEER THEORY and Sexual Identity

Queer theory, heavily influenced by both deconstruction and postmodernism, is a late 20th-century development in the field of critical theory.

It addresses itself to the nature of sexual identity. In **Judith Butler**'s (b. 1956) words, it attempts "to destabilize the entire system of sex regulation", and "binary oppositions such as gay/straight". Butler herself has promoted the idea of gender as "performance": "a kind of impersonation", as she puts it.

My argument is that personal identity is a very fluid notion with no "centre" or "essence" to it.

Butler

Hence Butler's diatribe against the "compulsory heterosexuality" of our society.

CUT ROUND OUTLINE & PASTE ON STAND

BASE

Butler is understandably attracted to such phenomena as "drag", in which gender identity is openly challenged.

Drag implicitly reveals the imitative structure of gender itself – as well as its contingency.

CUT ROUND OUTLINE

FOLD BACK TABS

Queer theory can be seen as an attempt to break away from the essentialist arguments of much feminist thought. In fact, it deliberately sets out to cultivate dialogue, and a sense of common interests, between lesbians and gay men.

In this instance at least, separatism is not on the agenda.

159

Black Criticism

Black criticism is another recent development in critical theory with a specific political agenda to pursue. Like feminist criticism, it is much concerned to create an alternative canon of writing, this time based on black writers.

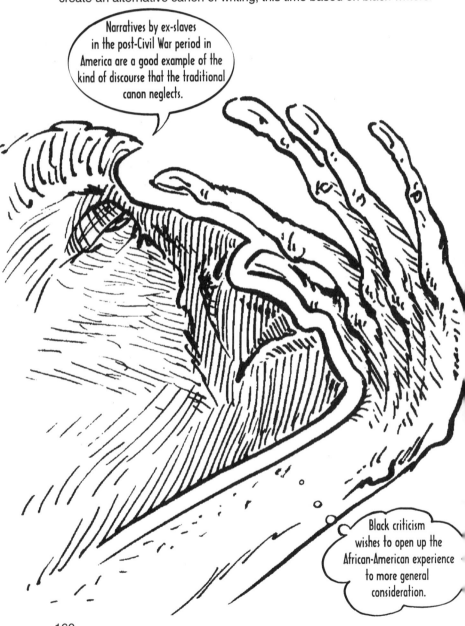

One of the most influential figures in this movement has been **Henry Louis Gates, Jr.** (b. 1950). He draws extensively on poststructuralism and postmodernism in his writings on the African-American literary tradition. In *The Signifying Monkey* (1988), Gates argues that there is often a hidden discourse within black writing itself.

It is often a case of authors "saying one thing" to mean "something quite other".

That's to protect ourselves from further oppression by the white authorities.

In this sense, the novelist <u>Ralph Ellison</u> (1914–94) wrote memorably of the "invisible black".

Black Feminist Criticism

Another theorist to make use of poststructuralist–postmodernist thought in this critical area of discourse has been the black feminist **bell hooks** (b. 1952). In her best-known book, *Ain't I a Woman* (1981), hooks points out that black women are doubly discriminated against culturally.

When black people are talked about, the focus tends to be on black men ...

When women are talked about, the focus tends to be on white women.

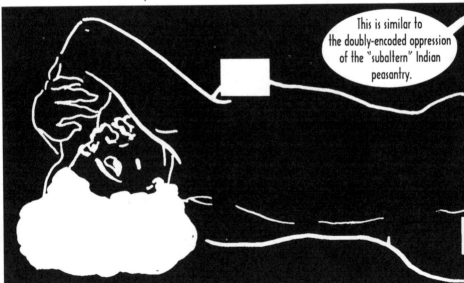

This is similar to the doubly-encoded oppression of the "subaltern" Indian peasantry.

Black female experience is seen to be yet another suppressed discourse which needs to be teased out by the critic. Taking inspiration from postmodern theory, hooks calls for the construction of a "politics of difference" in which "multiple black identities" can be allowed to express themselves.

Postmodernism tells us that there is no more an essential "black" identity than there is any other kind.

Critical Theory and a Pluralist World

Critical theory is an innately pluralist exercise. It presents us with a range of possible methods and perspectives by which to analyse not only cultural artefacts but also their *contexts* – social, political, historical, gender, ethnic. Pluralism is very much the current cultural paradigm in Western culture. Critical theory helps to reinforce this by fostering debate between various readings and "multiple interpretations".

The sheer diversity of positions possible within critical theory ...

OOOFF!
... bearing in mind its highly synthetic qualities – "Marxist feminism", "deconstructive feminism", "difference feminism" – and so on ...

DARK FORCES CULTURE SEXISM SLEAZE REPRESSION FEAR & LOATHING POWER CORRUPTION LIES PROFIT MONEY HEGEMONY GREED LUST OPPRESSION DOGMA CLASS RACISM EXPLOITATION

... argues against the development of any over-arching grand narrative for the time being.

In that sense, critical theory helps to promote the cause of democratic pluralism, and is therefore an integral part of the current political scene. **Theory is power.** This is not merely an academic exercise for "intellectual mandarins", but a perspective on awareness and a talent well worth developing for all of us.

165

Further Reading

The list below comprises some general introductions to critical theory and to key movements within the field.

Barry, Peter, **Beginning Theory: An Introduction to Literary and Cultural Theory** (Manchester: Manchester University Press, 1995). A well-organized, user-friendly survey of the major movements, with the emphasis on the literary side of things.

Culler, Jonathan, **Structuralist Poetics: Structuralism, Linguistics and the Study of Literature** (London and Henley: Routledge and Kegan Paul, 1975). Comprehensive study of structuralism that still holds up well over a quarter of a century later.

Eagleton, Terry, **Marxism and Literary Criticism** (London: Methuen, 1976). Solid and concise introduction to the field's most important figures and debates.

Gamble, Sarah, ed., **The Icon Critical Dictionary of Feminism and Postfeminism** (Cambridge: Icon Books, 1999; shortly to be republished by Routledge). Comprehensive study of the development of feminist thought and its impact on contemporary culture, complete with extensive glossary of key themes and figures.

Moi, Toril, **Sexual/Textual Politics: Feminist Literary Theory** (London: Methuen, 1985). One of the first attempts in English to capture the full range of feminist literary theory, with coverage of both Anglo-American and French approaches.

Norris, Christopher, **The Deconstructive Turn** (London: Methuen, 1983). Spirited defence of the value of deconstruction, in particular the work of Derrida.

Sarup, Madan, **An Introductory Guide to Post-Structuralism and Postmodernism** (Hemel Hempstead: Harvester, 1988). Clear exposition of the major concerns of these movements, with particular reference to the thought of Lacan, Derrida and Foucault.

Selden, Raman, and Widdowson, Peter, **A Reader's Guide to Contemporary Literary Theory** (Harvester: Hemel Hempstead, 1993 (revised edition)). Highly regarded general introduction, much used in literature degrees.

Sim, Stuart, ed., **The Icon Critical Dictionary of Postmodern Thought** (Cambridge: Icon Books, 1998; shortly to be republished by Routledge). Comprehensive study of the impact of postmodernism on the major discourses of Western culture, with an extensive glossary of the major concepts and figures involved in postmodernism's development.

Sim, Stuart, **Post-Marxism: An Intellectual History** (London: Routledge, 2000). Wide-ranging account of the development of dissenting trends within Marxism, from the movement's early stages through to the emergence of post-Marxism.

Sim, Stuart, 'Structuralism and Post-structuralism' and 'Marxism and Aesthetics', in Oswald Hanfling, ed., **Philosophical Aesthetics: An Introduction** (Oxford: Blackwell, 1992), pp. 405–39 and 441–71. Two historically-based essays outlining the major concepts and concerns in structuralist, poststructuralist and Marxist critical theory.

166

Glossary of Terms

Alienation: Many modern thinkers and artists have claimed that a sense of alienation from other human beings is the natural human condition. Marx, on the other hand, argued that individuals were alienated from each other by the dehumanizing processes of industrial labour.

Archaeology: Michel Foucault's term for his historical researches into the hidden discourses of Western society (such as its suppressed history of homosexuality). The aim of these archaeologies was to show that Western culture was based on power relations rather than such idealistic notions as truth or natural justice.

Aura: According to Walter Benjamin, the unique quality which differentiates a work of art from its reproduction. A critical factor in the development of this aura is the cultural history of the artefact itself – its sense of belonging to a certain tradition.

Base/Superstructure: In classical Marxist theory, society is made up of an economic base or infrastructure and a superstructure which comprises all other human social and cultural activities. The base is held to dictate the form that those various activities – religion, the law, politics, education, the media, the arts, etc. – will take.

Body-without-organs: The term used by Gilles Deleuze and Felix Guattari to describe the complex of forces in our society which strive to repress the expression of individual desire. Capital, for example, is treated as the body-without-organs of the capitalist.

Carnival: Mikhail Bakhtin saw the institution of carnival as a model for subversion of socio-political authority in the way that it parodied the ruling class. The comic genius Rabelais was for Bakhtin an excellent example of the application of the carnival spirit to literary narrative.

Chaos theory: Chaos theory emphasizes how sensitive systems are to changes in their initial conditions, and how unpredictable this makes their behaviour. One of the most disturbing aspects of the theory is that it allows for the simultaneous presence of randomness and determinism within systems.

Class consciousness: The sense of belonging to a specific social class, whose common interests create a sense of solidarity in its members. Marxists believe that when the proletariat, for example, reaches an awareness of its exploited status, then there is the basis for a social revolution.

Complexity theory: Complexity theory argues that physical systems can evolve to higher levels of development through spontaneous self-organization. This phenomenon can be seen at work in organisms as diverse as human consciousness or the entire universe – possibly even within the more sophisticated computer networks.

Compulsory heterosexuality: The contention that heterosexuality is viewed as the sexual norm in Western societies, with all other sexual practices being treated as deviations. Michel Foucault, Judith Butler and the queer theory movement have argued that this inhibits the full expression of our sexual natures.

167

Critical realism: Georg Lukács's term for literary narratives that demonstrate how the economic system forms human character. In the case of capitalism, this is assumed to encourage the development of competitiveness and self-interest. Lukács did not require the author to condemn this practice, merely make it apparent to the reader.

Cyborg: The combination of human and machine (the term is a contraction of "cybernetic organism"). In the work of Donna Haraway, this notion is celebrated as a way of escaping human, and most particularly gender, limitations.

Death of the author: A concept devised by Roland Barthes to describe the process by which texts take on a life of their own after they leave the author. Henceforth, they become the province of the reader, who is in no way bound by whatever the author's intentions may have been.

Deep structure: In structuralist theory, systems are held to have deep structures which dictate how they operate. Roland Barthes, for example, assumed an underlying structure of rules to narrative. Another way of thinking of deep structure is as something similar to a genetic programme.

Defamiliarization: The process by which literary language renders the everyday unfamiliar to the reader. By "making strange" the aspects of our world, authors force us to notice what we normally take for granted. The concept was coined by Viktor Shklovsky.

Desiring machine: Gilles Deleuze and Felix Guattari see individual human beings as motivated by the need to find an outlet for their libidinal energy: in their terminology, as "desiring-machines". Much of modern society, in their view, is dedicated to suppressing this drive.

Deterritorialization: Gilles Deleuze and Felix Guattari regard institutional authority as inherently territorial in mentality. Attempts to contest the boundaries that institutions set therefore count as acts of deterritorialization. Nomadic thought (q.v.) is an example of such transgressive behaviour.

Dialectical materialism: In the Hegelian dialectic, thesis generates antithesis, with the conflict between the two resolving itself into the creation of a new thesis or synthesis. Marx took over this scheme, but located it in the material world where it manifested itself in the struggle of one class against another. Resolution would come about in our own era when the proletariat overcame the bourgeoisie.

Dialogism: Mikhail Bakhtin conceived of meaning as in a constant process of negotiation between individuals in a given society; that is, as "dialogic". Rather than being fixed, meaning is plural and always open to reinterpretation – and the same can be said of any narrative.

Différance: The neologism coined by Jacques Derrida to describe the way in which words fail to achieve fixed meaning at any one point. Meaning is always indeterminate to Derrida – both "differed" and "deferred" – and *différance* is the movement within language that prevents it from being otherwise.

Difference: In poststructuralist and postmodernist thought, difference is always emphasized over unity, and is taken to be an inescapable aspect of human affairs.

168

Systems, and texts, are held to be internally marked by difference and incapable of achieving unity: rather, they lend themselves to multiple interpretations.

Differend: Jean-François Lyotard's term for an irresolvable dispute, in which each side starts from incommensurable premises. An employer and an employee debating employment rights would be one example; colonizer and colonized debating property rights another. Traditionally, what happens is that the stronger side imposes its will on the weaker.

Discourse: In the work of Michel Foucault, discourse constitutes a social practice governed by an agreed set of conventions. Medicine is a discourse, as is law, or any academic discipline. Discourses are founded on power relations, and function something like paradigms (q.v.) in Thomas Kuhn.

Double coding: Charles Jencks's term to describe how postmodern architecture ought to work; that is, to appeal to both a specialist and a general audience. Modernist architecture had signally failed to do so, in his opinion, restricting its appeal to specialist practitioners only.

Écriture féminine: French feminists such as Hèléne Cixous and Luce Irigaray have argued that women should develop a style of writing uniquely their own, self-consciously distancing themselves from patriarchal modes of expression. Other than a certain fluidity of meaning, however, it is difficult to specify what the style actually involves.

Enlightenment project: The cultural movement, dating from the Enlightenment period in the 18th century, that emphasizes the role of reason in human affairs and is committed to material progress and the liberation of humankind from political servitude. Modern culture is based on these premises.

Epic theatre: A theory of drama developed by the playwright Bertolt Brecht which demanded that, rather than providing an illusion of real life, theatre should make its artifice visible by "alienation effect" to the audience. Theatre that did so, Brecht thought, would then become a critique of the dominant values of its society.

Grand narrative: In the work of Jean-François Lyotard, a grand narrative constitutes a universal explanatory theory which admits no substantial opposition to its principles. Marxism is one such example, liberal humanism another, with ideology in general tending to operate in such an authoritarian manner.

Gynocriticism: According to Elaine Showalter, the proper object of feminist critics is texts that concentrate on female experience, or "gynotexts". The concern of gynocriticism is to trace the development of a specifically female literary tradition, thus challenging patriarchal accounts of literary history.

Hegemony: In Marxist theory (particularly the work of Antonio Gramsci), hegemony explains how the ruling class exerts domination over all other classes by a variety of apparent "consensus" means, including the use of the media to transmit its system of values.

Heroinism: Literature by female authors in which the female protagonists are placed in situations which test their characters and require them to display heroic behaviour in order to survive. The term was devised by Ellen Moers, for whom 18th-century Gothic novels were an example of "travelling heroinism".

Heteroglossia: Mikhail Bakhtin's term to describe the intertextual (q.v.) nature of novels. The novel is a very flexible and open form, capable of referring to a multitude of cultural discourses. Bakhtin saw this as subversive since it resisted the unifying (that is, conservative) forces operating within most cultures.

Homology: Lucien Goldmann's work explores the way in which literary texts can express the world view of certain influential social groups contemporary with those texts. There is, in other words, a "homology" between text and group, with the former articulating the latter's beliefs more clearly than they can.

Hybridity: The concept of hybridity figures large in postcolonial theory. For Homi K. Bhabha, it represents a condition between states (somewhere between working-class identity and gender, for example) whose virtue is that it escapes the control of either. As such, it has considerable subversive potential.

Hyperreality: Jean Baudrillard's concept to describe the condition beyond meaning that, for him, sums up postmodern life. A cultural phenomenon like Disneyland no longer means anything: it is neither the real thing nor a representation of the past. Rather, it is hyperreal – beyond meaning or analysis.

Ideological State Apparatus: Louis Althusser's term for all those institutions, such as the legal and educational systems, the arts and the media, which serve to transmit and reinforce the values of the dominant ideology.

Imaginary: In Lacanian theory, the pre-self conscious state of young babies aged up to six months or so. Lacan identifies this state with the mother, and we leave it when we move into the symbolic (q.v.) realm of language and social existence at the age of around eighteen months.

Inhuman: For Jean-François Lyotard, all those processes which conspire to marginalize the human dimension in our world. Examples would include the growth of computerization, and particularly the development of sophisticated, and eventually autonomous, systems of Artificial Intelligence and Artificial Life.

Interpellation: The process by which ideology manipulates us to conform to its values. For Louis Althusser, it was a case of ideology "hailing" us, almost like a policeman calling us to attention. We respond to such signs in reflex fashion, thus revealing how successfully ideology has conditioned us.

Interpretive community: For Stanley Fish, an interpretive community constitutes the body of scholars working in a critical discipline whose collective practices set the criteria for interpretation. These practices can change over time, and the community might be thought of as similar to Thomas Kuhn's concept of paradigm (q.v.).

Intertextuality: A term which describes the way in which all texts echo other texts, and are, as theorists such as Mikhail Bakhtin and Julia Kristeva have pointed out, "mosaics of quotations" and references from an extensive variety of sources.

Linguistic model: Ferdinand de Saussure's model of how language works – a system with its own internally consistent rules or grammar – was appropriated by he structuralist movement which applied it to any and all phenomena. The main concern of structuralist analysis then became to isolate and catalogue the grammar of whatever system was being studied.

Literariness: The quality that differentiates literary language from other forms of language-use. This quality largely derives from the highly self-conscious use of literary devices in literary texts, and according to Roman Jakobson is the proper object of study of literary critics.

Little narrative: The opposite to grand narrative (q.v.), little narratives comprise groups of like-minded individuals who attempt to subvert the power of grand narratives. Little narratives remain at an oppositional level and refuse to allow themselves to be turned into authoritarian ideologies of the kind they are rejecting.

Metanarrative: Another name for grand narrative (q.v.). Jean-François Lyotard uses the terms interchangeably in his best-known work, *The Postmodern Condition* (1979).

Metaphysics of presence: Jacques Derrida argues that all discourse in Western culture is based on the assumption that the full meanings of words are immediately present to us, in our minds, as we use them. For Derrida, this "metaphysics of presence" is illusory: meaning is always indeterminate.

Narratology: The study of how narrative works in terms of the relations between its structural elements. Structuralists like Barthes, in their desire to establish a general grammar of narrative, reduced narrative to a set of functions, specifying how these applied in each literary genre.

Negative dialectics: Both the Hegelian and Marxist dialectic feature a conflict between thesis and antithesis which resolves itself into the creation of a new thesis. For Theodor Adorno, however, the dialectic failed to resolve its internal contradictions, with new theses simply starting another cycle of conflict. Dialectics were negative rather than positive in quality.

Nomadism: Thought which does not follow established patterns or respect traditional boundaries (such as disciplinary ones). For Gilles Deleuze and Felix Guattari, nomadism is a transgressive activity which challenges institutional authority, given that the latter is invariably committed to protecting its own particular "territory".

Orientalism: Edward Said's term for the way in which the Middle East has been constructed (by writers and artists, for example) as the "other" to Western culture. In the process, the "Orient" is presented as mysterious, sensuous and irrational: qualities which tend to be looked down upon in the West.

Paganism: Jean-François Lyotard argued that paganism was the state in which judgements were reached without reference to pre-existing rules and conventions, but on a "case by case" basis instead. Judgement in any one case established no precedent for another.

Paradigm: A framework of thought which dictates what counts as acceptable inquiry in an intellectual field. Thomas Kuhn saw scientific history as consisting of a series of paradigms, each incommensurable with its predecessor, with periodic revolutions when one paradigm replaced another.

Pluralism: The commitment to multiple interpretations and the rejection of the notion of an unquestionable central authority, whether in critical or political matters. Pluralists refuse to privilege any one interpretation of a text or ideological position, and encourage diversity.

Readerly fiction: Roland Barthes's term for fiction which imposes a particular reading of the text on the reader, and attempts to close off alternative interpretations. 19th-century novelistic realism, with its carefully worked-out plots and explicit moral messages, is a prime example of this style of writing.

Reception theory: Reception theorists concentrate on the interaction of reader and text (reader-response being another name for the approach). Textual meaning is seen to emerge from the reader's engagement with the text, with some theorists claiming that the reader is almost entirely responsible for the creation of that meaning.

Reflection theory: Reflection theorists assume that artistic artefacts reflect the ideology of their culture. Thus, for the Marxist Georgi Plekhanov, the art of a bourgeois culture could not help but reveal the character of that culture. Art has a rather passive cultural role from this perspective.

Repressive State Apparatus: Louis Althusser's term for those forces, such as the police and the army, which the ruling class relies on to enforce its control over a society – by violent means if necessary.

Rhizome: For Gilles Deleuze and Felix Guattari, the rhizome became a model for how systems ideally should develop. Rhizomatic structures (such as tubers or moss) can make connections between any two points on their surface; a process which these thinkers considered to be inherently creative and anti-authoritarian.

Schizoanalysis: Gilles Deleuze and Felix Guattari's attack on Freudian psychoanalysis led them to develop the concept of schizoanalysis, in which schizophrenia was taken as a model of how to resist the methods of the psychoanalyst. The multiple personalities of the schizophrenic frustrated the psychoanalytic desire to turn us into socially conformist individuals.

Seduction: Jean Baudrillard's method for subverting systems is based on the notion of "seducing" or "beguiling" them into submission, rather than resorting to the more usual means of overt political action or revolution.

Semiology: Ferdinand de Saussure predicted the development of semiology – "the science of signs" – in his *Course in General Linguistics* (1916). Language itself, in Saussure's formulation, was a system of signs (q.v.) which operated according to an underlying grammar. All sign-systems were assumed to work on this linguistic model.

Semiotics: Although it is sometimes used interchangeably with semiology (q.v.) to mean "the science of signs", semiotics has also come to refer to the operation of signs in a given system. Thus, one speaks of the semiotics of film or fashion.

Sign/Signified/Signifier: For Ferdinand de Saussure, language is made up of signs, which consist of an arbitrary signifier (word) and a signified (concept) joined in n act of understanding in the individual's mind. The sign communicates meaning, which in Saussurean linguistics is held to be a relatively stable entity.

imulacra: According to Jean Baudrillard, signs no longer represent some deeper r hidden meaning (such as the class struggle), but only themselves. We live now in world of simulations which *have* no deeper meaning to be discovered. Disneyland s a good example of such a simulation.

ocialist realism: An aesthetic theory imposed on artists in the Soviet Union from ne early 1930s onwards. This demanded that works of art appeal to a popular udience and, where possible (as in the visual and literary arts), contain an explicit ocialist message.

trange attractor: In chaos theory, the underlying force which controls any given ystem. The weather, for example, is assumed to have a strange attractor which ictates its patterns. The most extreme example of a strange attractor is a black ole, which absorbs all matter with which it comes into contact.

ubaltern: To be in the subaltern position is to be in an inferior position culturally, nus subject to oppression by groups more powerfully placed within the dominant leology (as women so often are by men, or the colonized by their colonizers).

ymbolic: In Lacanian theory, the state that succeeds the imaginary (q.v.) at around ighteen months in a child's life. The symbolic is the realm of language and social xistence. Lacan identifies it with the "masculine" world of adulthood. Feminists see nis as the entry into repression.

Vomanism: Theories which assume the superiority of women. The term suggests reverse kind of sexism in which the prejudice always lies with the woman's osition.

Vriterly fiction: Roland Barthes's term for fiction which does not impose a particular eading of a text on the reader, and which invites alternative interpretations. In arthes's canon, modernism is the style of writing that best achieves this desirable bjective.

The Author

Stuart Sim is Professor of English Studies at the University of Sunderland. His books include *Derrida and the End of History* and *Lyotard and the Inhuman* in Icon's 'Postmodern Encounters' series.

The Illustrator

Borin Van Loon has illustrated more hot dinners than you have eaten books. He has given physical form to *Darwin and Evolution, Genetics, Buddha, Eastern Philosophy, Sociology, Cultural Studies, Mathematics* and *Media Studies* in Icon's 'Introducing' series.

Index